Richard Wright's Art of Tragedy

Richard Wright's
Art of Tragedy

By Joyce Ann Joyce

 University of Iowa Press
Iowa City

University of Iowa Press, Iowa City 52242
Printed in the United States of America
Second printing, 1987

Jacket and book design by Joanna Hill
Typesetting by G & S Typesetters, Austin, Texas
Printing and binding by Thomson-Shore, Dexter, Michigan

Library of Congress Cataloging-in-Publication Data

Joyce, Joyce Ann, 1949–
    Richard Wright's art of tragedy.

    Bibliography: p.
    Includes index.
    1. Wright, Richard, 1908–1960. Native son.
2. Afro-Americans in literature.   3. Tragic, The, in
literature.   I. Title.
PS3545.R815N34   1986   813'.52   86-6906
ISBN 0-87745-148-6

For my parents,

Henry and Edna Joyce

At the still point of the turning world. Neither flesh nor fleshless;
Neither from nor towards; at the still point, there the dance is,
But neither arrest nor movement. And do not call it fixity,
Where past and future are gathered. Neither movement from nor
   towards,
Neither ascent nor decline. Except for the point, the still point,
There would be no dance, and there is only the dance.

From "Burnt Norton" in T. S.
Eliot's *Four Quartets*

Contents

Acknowledgments

Time and support for the initial stage of research were provided by a Graduate Research Award I received from the University of Maryland in the summer of 1980; the university's General Research Board also provided a Book Subsidy Award to assist with publication. Yet, without the generosity of a rather large number of friends, I do not know how I would have acquired the time and serenity I needed to complete this book. Thus I shall always be grateful for the "personal grants" I received from my brother Ralph Joyce, Professor Rodney Baine, Professor Dorothy Graham, Marie Davidson, Professor Eugene Hammond, Professor Linda Merians, Betty Fern, Julia Freelove Blondet, Professor Neil Isaacs, Carolyn and Hank Parks, Professor Theresa Coletti, and Steve and Mary Freelove, Georgiana and Roy Harvey, and Susie Harper.

I would like to thank Betty Fern and Beatriz Dailey for the long hours of typing and for their patience in helping me meet deadlines. Beth Alvarez was also quite generous with the hours she spent proofreading the manuscript twice.

I am especially grateful to Lisa McCullough for editing the manuscript and for her faith and encouragement. And finally, not only did Professor Michel Fabre critique the manuscript in its very early stages, but he also provided me with the diverse professional support I needed to mature as a scholar and teacher.

Prologue

pproximately eleven years ago, my major professor in the English department at the University of Georgia handed me a copy of Richard Wright's *Native Son*. I was instantly entranced by Bigger Thomas. I read everything the library at the University of Georgia had to offer by and about Richard Wright. On a surface level, it might appear that the University of Georgia system had done virtually nothing to prepare me for a career in Black American literary criticism. The English department, at the time I was there, offered only one undergraduate course in Black American literature. But I was quite lucky: like Wright, I had my own equivalent to the white Catholic with the library card—my major professor, Dr. William Free, a Tennessean who suggested that I use Wright's works as the subject for all my seminar reports and term papers in his classes. We both intuitively agreed that Wright would be the subject of my dissertation. Engrossed by the stylistic similarities between Wright's last novel, *The Long Dream*, and his first published novel, *Native Son*, I stopped searching for a topic. In August 1979, I completed my dissertation, which was entitled "Richard Wright's *The Long Dream*: An Aesthetic Extension of *Native Son*."

I wrote to Michel Fabre at the Sorbonne, asking him to read my work and engaging in an exchange of ideas that resulted in the present book, which is conceptually more precise and significantly different from my dissertation. At first I was taken aback, even a little stunned, by his idea that what I had found suggested that *Native Son* was a tragedy and *The Long Dream* a *Bildungsroman*. It was well over a year after our correspondence had begun that I settled on a thesis for a book on Wright.

In an age that was excitedly discovering the role of women in the works of Black women writers, that was focusing on folklore in Ralph Ellison and in Richard Wright, that was focusing on "Narration, Authentication, and Authorial Control in Frederick Douglass' Narrative of 1845," and on "Preface to Blackness: Text and Pretext," I turned for guidance to the great works of literary criticism. As soon as I began to reread Aristotle's *Poetics*, I was bombarded with parallels between the art of tragedy as Aristotle defined it and *Native Son*. The more I read, the more I was convinced of my thesis: *Native Son* is a tragedy, according to traditional definitions.

Trained by professors who were almost all southerners—many educated at Vanderbilt—and descendants of the Agrarian or New Critical school of literary theory, I am faithful to a close reading of the text. I distrust content until I discover how the language of a work conjoins with the message as interdependent conspirators that create the power inherent in the work. Very little—in many cases nothing—in the critical commentaries on Wright's novels justifies the commonly held views that *Native Son* is a great novel and *The Long Dream* and *Savage Holiday* are disappointing failures. As I teach *Native Son* every semester in the English department at the University of Maryland and as I continue to read many works of Black American literature, what once looked like three distinct problems converge now as one. Robert Stepto and Dexter Fisher's edition of *Afro-American Literature: The Reconstruction of Instruction*, published in 1979 by the Modern Language Association, demonstrated that the sociological school that had dominated the criticism of Black writers was being replaced by some strange school that isolated language from social institutions. After reading the essays in this volume, I began to understand the interrelationship of class, culture, and ideology.

It was no cultural accident that the first works of Black American literature—the slave narratives, the folk poetry, *Clotel*, *Our Nig*—focused on the institution of slavery. This response of the Black American writer to his environment is still a reflection of how the writer interprets his or her relationship to the mainstream culture. The earlier works of Black American literary criticism— including the works of Du Bois, Braithwaite, and later Richard Wright—all shaped their literary standards after white models. Even when the subject matter of their novels and criticism condemns racism, as is the case with Wright's "The Literature of the Negro in the United States," the technique reflects the accepted traditions of the white literary mainstream. It is quite natural that Henry Gates's and Robert Stepto's indoctrination into the poststructuralist school of literary thought follows the cultural and political upheavals of the 1960s. The literary and political spokespersons of the 1960s movement are now themselves either surprisingly obscure or still committed to the progress of Black people safely working within the confines of a middle-class structure. Both Julius Wilson's *The Declining Significance of Race* (1978) and Thomas Sowell's *Ethnic America* (1981) are more reflections of a Black elitist class structure than of a decline in the significance of race. The educational and social changes that characterize the lives of Black Americans in the 1980s point to the existence of a Black elite in which two generations of college-educated Blacks live in the same home.

Consequently, it is also quite natural that these educated Blacks manifest both the influences of their Black cultural heritage and those of the exogamic, epistemological training of their educational experiences. And, of course, historically one of the most elitist components of the humanities has been the field of literary criticism. I suppose it is safe to assert that literary criticism, whether it be Aristotelian, historical, New Critical, structuralist, or poststructuralist, is inherently pseudoscientific. For the essential element of literary criticism is analysis. And the peculiar combinations of methodology and epistemology differentiate one school of criticism from another. A critic's preference for a particular school is molded by the collective influences of the times in which he or she writes as well as by his or her educational environment. Thus the elitism that characterizes the reconstructionist Black literary theory is a subgroup of the same exclusive literary theories that now dominate the academic literary scene.

We have come a long way since Joyce's *Finnegans Wake* and Henry James's introduction to American literature of the third-person limited narrative point of view, which is designed to approximate the intricacies and limitations of human thought and interaction. The structural intricacies of Thomas Pynchon's *Gravity's Rainbow* and Beckett's persistent, ongoing determination to strip reality of all meaning represent our twentieth-century obsession with obscurity, indecision, and fear of the finite. Contemporary literary criticism now rests on the far extreme from that of the Aristotelian school. For implicit in Aristotle's *Poetics* is the assumption of the interdependence of art and life. The Agrarian or New Critical school shared with Aristotle and Greek culture a faith or certainty concerning what the world should be like. Thus the Agrarians could in good conscience isolate the art form under analysis from its social, political, and biographical contexts.

Richard Wright, too, had a strong faith in what he believed the world should be like. Because of his unflinching dedication to enlightening mankind and because of the enigmatic power of his art, no other Black American writer has attracted as much attention as Wright. Even the curricula in mainstream English departments that traditionally exclude Blacks include at least one of his works, most often *Native Son*. So far, the laurels of literary criticism have bestowed upon Wright a dubious honor. From studying most of the criticism on Wright to date, a student of literature will get a sure grasp of Wright's Mississippi cultural heritage; his relationship to his mother, father, grandmother, and other relatives; his difficulty in acquiring an education; the chronological sequence of his works; the relationship between his travels and his works; and most importantly, the social and political ideology that governs the interaction between his characters. The student does not get a sense of Wright's artistry. This failure to address the creativity that underlies Wright's craft epitomizes the problem that defines the present state of Black American literary analyses.

It is discouraging to note that Black American literary criticism has reached its poststructuralist stage without having undergone the rigorous historical examination that illuminates the poetics or sublimity of other great works of literature. It has skipped a whole phase in the evolution of literary criticism. The natural cycle presupposes that a school of literary thought be created from the one that came before. Hence the move from sociological, biographical criticism to poststructuralist theories means that the reconstructionist/poststructuralist principles are being applied in a historical vacuum. What I attempt to do in the chapters that follow is to begin to fill that gap, focusing specifically on the stylistic characteristics of Wright's most successful novel to show how his language merges with his subject matter to illuminate *Native Son* as a tragedy.

I do not mean to suggest that I will provide a conservative, formal, New Critical reading. To do so would seriously undermine Wright's purpose. Yet, as I pointed out earlier, having been trained by the disciples of Agrarians, I have always had a keen interest in what makes a novel work, what makes it move, what makes it endure. A simple chart that I use to attract the attention of my students illustrates the essential paradoxes of *Native Son*:

MOMENTS OF SILENCE		MOMENTS OF ANGER
\		/
PERIODS OF ABSTRACT BROODING		PERIODS OF INTENSE DESIRE
\		/
INDIFFERENCE (WALL)		VIOLENCE (LEAP TO ACTION)
\		/
	BIGGER	
/		\
HERO		MURDERER
\		/
SUN (YELLOW)		SNOW
\		/
BLACK (ENTRAPMENT FEAR HUMILIATION)		WHITE (DANGER BLINDNESS INSENSITIVITY)

This diagram manifests the parallels between the dialectical characteristics of the images and symbols and the duality inherent in Bigger's psyche. Because tragedy concerns itself with ambiguity in the personality of the hero and with irony in the events that affect the hero's life, it is important that we transcend the conceptions of Bigger as a naturalistic victim limited by the strictures of his environment. For this reason, Chapter 1 attempts to show the commonality among naturalism, existentialism, and tragedy as well as their points of demarcation, while Chapters 2 and 3 examine respectively the nature of Bigger's environment and his personality traits from the point of view of tragedy. These three chapters prepare the way for Chapter 4, which shows how Wright's ingenious use of language captures the tragic vision through its illumination of the dichotomies responsible for the tension in Bigger's life. Chapter 5 illustrates the processes by which Wright synthesizes these dichotomies.

Still suffering from the detached effects of New Criticism and living in the midst of a poststructuralist critical age, we tend to forget that the *how* of a world created in a work of fiction is inextricably melded to the *what*. Neither exists without the other. Of course, the symbolic and larger stylistic patterns in *Native Son* grow out of Wright's being an American in general and a Black American in particular. These patterns are a result of his particular sensibility and experiences. However, it is not Wright's experiences that are highlighted when we read *Native Son*, but Bigger's.

Finally, unlike the scholarship on Ralph Ellison's *Invisible Man*, the critical commentaries on Wright begin with a comprehensive perspective and have yet to concentrate on detail. The analyses of Ellison's *Invisible Man* address more immediately the forms that underlie his artistry. Robert O'Meally's excellent *The Craft of Ralph Ellison* (1982) skillfully begins with a broad view of biography and sensibility and then moves inward, showing how these forces shape Ellison's use of folklore in his art, particularly in *Invisible Man*. My goals are necessarily different from O'Meally's. Just as not enough has been known about Ellison's well-protected

personal life, too much is known of Wright's life. This book shifts
the emphasis from biography to the artistic vision and masterful crafting of Wright's major work. I have tried to provide—for
the first time in a full-length study—a means by which students
and teachers can firmly grasp the stylistic genius that marks *Native Son*.

Richard Wright's Art of Tragedy

1. The Critical Background and a New Perspective

In his essay aptly titled "The 'Fate' Section of *Native Son*," Edward Kearns, in a discussion of courses in Afro-American literature, summarizes the "fate" of criticism written on the works of Black literary artists: ". . . black American writers have been nearly excluded from serious critical attention, and when attention has been paid, the black American writer has generally been treated as an author of social documents rather than works of art" (149). No criticism on the works of a Black writer demonstrates the validity of Kearns's statement more than that written on Richard Wright's *Native Son*. The immediate impact of *Native Son* elevated Wright to the position of father of Black American literature, changed the course of Black American fiction, and attracted the attention of literary circles all over the world. First published in 1940, *Native Son* is continually translated from English into other languages: Czech, 1947; Danish, 1959; Dutch, 1947; Finnish, 1972; French, 1947; Georgian, 1971; German, 1941; Italian, 1948; Japanese, 1972; Norwegian, 1947; Polish, 1969; Portuguese, 1949; Rumanian, 1954; Russian, 1941; Spanish, 1941; Swedish, 1943; and Turkish, 1975.

The attention given the novel on American soil is equally striking. A brief survey of the best-known studies of Wright substantiates Kearns's view of the state of Black American literary criticism by showing that most studies dealing with Wright's canon discuss his recurring themes and his life, but not his art. Those who have written single studies devoted to Wright and whose names appear frequently are Edward Margolies, Dan McCall, Robert Bone, Russell Brignano, Keneth Kinnamon, and most recently Michel Fabre. The year 1969 marks the appearance of three significant additions to criticism on Wright: Margolies's *The Art of Richard Wright*, McCall's *The Example of Richard Wright*, and Bone's pamphlet *Richard Wright*. Although these studies are heavily biographical, Margolies, Brignano, and Kinnamon directed significant attention to Wright's works within their established frameworks. Still, despite the promising title, Margolies's work is disappointing, for in this single study he includes a chapter on *Black Boy* and *Twelve Million Black Voices* (Wright's pictorial history of the Black man in America), a chapter on *Black Power* and *Pagan Spain*, a chapter on *The Color Curtain* and *White Man, Listen!*, a chapter on *Uncle Tom's Children* and *Eight Men*, a chapter on *Lawd Today*, a chapter on *Native Son*, a chapter on *The Outsider* and *Savage Holiday*, and finally a chapter on *The Long Dream*. The list is almost as extensive as Wright's canon. Brignano's study *Richard Wright: An Introduction to the Man and His Works* is primarily ideological, concentrating on Marxism, Wright's affiliation with the Communist party, and the philosophical premises that shaped Wright's thought. In *The Emergence of Richard Wright*, Keneth Kinnamon's concern is *Native Son*; thus his earlier chapters function as background material for *Native Son*. His first two chapters are "The Burdens of Caste and Class" and "Wright's Literary Apprenticeship"; the second chapter includes comments on Wright's proletarian poems that introduce his radical ideology. In addition, while this study was in its final stages, the University of Mississippi Press published Michel Fabre's *The World of Richard Wright* (1985). This collection of twelve of Fabre's previously published essays presents a diverse look at the broad range of influences on Wright's creative imagination.

Not as well known as Margolies, Kinnamon, Brignano, and Fabre, David Bakish, Milton and Patricia Rickels, and Katherine Fishburn are the authors of three other books whose sole subject is Richard Wright. Like Bone's pamphlet, the Rickelses' study *Richard Wright*, published in 1970 by the Southern Writers Series, merely provides a biographical sketch and a critical reading of most of Wright's canon in forty-two pages! More useful than this study is Bakish's *Richard Wright*, published in 1973. Although Bakish makes perceptive critical comments, his work is primarily a biography, dividing Wright's life into three periods: his experiences in Mississippi and Chicago, in New York, and in Paris. Of all the fairly recent studies of Wright (including Robert Felgar's *Richard Wright*, 1980), Katherine Fishburn's *Richard Wright's Hero: The Faces of a Rebel-Victim*, published in 1977 and originally a Michigan State University dissertation, is the most impressive. It is a thematic, philosophical study of the protagonists of all of Wright's novels except *Savage Holiday*. This esoteric look at Wright's ideological and philosophical influences includes numerous references to Freud, Frye, Hassan, Sartre, Camus, Nietzsche, Dostoevski, and Booth. Obviously, Fishburn is not concerned primarily with the minute techniques of Wright's artistry. And Felgar's *Richard Wright*, a publication of the Twayne's United States Authors Series which follows a restricted format, limits itself exclusively to the traditional format which characterizes works in such a series and only repeats many of the already well-established interpretations of Wright's works.

In addition to the texts devoted solely to Wright, a large number of books contain individual chapters or major sections on Wright's works. Any list of the most well known of these would have to include Carl Milton Hughes's *The Negro Novelists 1940–1950* (1953), Walter Allen's *The Modern Novel* (1964), Harold Cruse's *The Crisis of the Negro Intellectual* (1967), Edward Margolies's *Native Sons: A Critical Study of Twentieth-Century Negro American Authors* (1968), C. W. E. Bigsby's *The Black American Writer* (1969), Donald B. Gibson's *Five Black Writers* (1970), A. Robert Lee's edition of *Black Fiction: New Studies in the Afro-American Novel Since 1945* (1980), and Donald B. Gibson's *The Politics of Literary Expression: A Study of Major Black Writers* (1981).

None of these studies devotes itself to a pointed discussion of Wright's artistry: they are largely biographical and sociological.

Margolies focuses heavily on *Native Son*, stating many of the same ideas as most of Wright's critics. *Native Son* is also the subject of Hughes's discussion of Wright. Hughes maintains that the psychological, sociological, and economic factors in *Native Son* influenced the Black novelists of the 1940s (68). Thus he, too, approaches Wright's work thematically. Walter Allen carries this thematic emphasis one step further by showing the "universality" of Wright's subject matter. In his summary of the history of the British and American novel from the 1920s to beyond World War II, Allen shows that the same social and economic conditions that precipitated *Studs Lonigan* and *The Grapes of Wrath* also anticipated *Native Son* (155–56). An historically significant study, Cruse's *The Crisis of the Negro Intellectual* concentrates on Wright's Marxist ideology and on Wright's delineation of this ideology in his "Blueprint for Negro Writing," published in the fall 1937 issue of *New Challenge*. Cruse asserts that Wright's Marxist ideology smothered his creative abilities (188). Much like Cruse's assessment of Wright's career, Warren French's "The Lost Potential of Richard Wright," found in C. W. E. Bigsby's first volume of *The Black American Writer*, holds that Wright's career as a serious artist ended with his departure for France (1:134). Donald Gibson's *Five Black Writers* collects six of the best-known essays on Wright. Although all of them are monumental studies, only Edwin Berry Burgum's "The Art of Richard Wright's Short Stories" addresses itself to Wright's artistry. Unfortunately, Burgum concludes that Wright's reputation as a stylist rests on the art of the short stories alone (37). Gibson's more recent *The Politics of Literary Expression* and A. Robert Lee's edition of *Black Fiction* both include one chapter on Richard Wright. The title of Gibson's chapter on Wright clearly illuminates the perspective he takes: "Richard Wright: The Politics of a Lone Marxian." Ian Walker's essay "Black Nightmare: The Fiction of Richard Wright," collected in Lee's text, sees Bigger Thomas's characterization in *Native Son* as a working out of "racial and psychological problems rather than political and economic" (23).

Too many scholars believe that Wright was at his best when he wrote out of the anger aroused by his experiences as a child in Mississippi and as a young man in Memphis, Chicago, and New York. This attitude finds its source in both the subject matter of Wright's novel and in the cultural conditions that have long separated the aesthetics that govern mainstream literature from those of Black American literature. The peculiar racial history shared by Black and white Americans, the concomitant view of Bigger Thomas as victim, Bigger's sensational murder of a white woman, and the numerous analogies between Bigger's life and Richard Wright's experiences bog *Native Son* down in sociological, thematic studies. In order to see beyond the worn lenses of biography, naturalism, and existentialism in our analyses of *Native Son*, it is necessary that we understand the basis for the old critical approach which links Wright's creativity to his life experiences.

This exploration begins with a look at the studies devoted to impressions and perspectives of Wright's personal life and with the four biographies to date. David Ray and Robert W. Farnsworth's *Richard Wright* is perhaps more objective than the personal views of Wright's friends Saunders Redding, Horace Cayton, and Arna Bontemps in *Anger, and Beyond*, edited by Herbert Hill. Of the four biographies, Michel Fabre's *The Unfinished Quest of Richard Wright* (1973) emerges as the most comprehensive in perspective. Unlike Constance Webb's *Richard Wright: A Biography* (1968) and John A. Williams's *The Most Native of Sons* (1970), *The Unfinished Quest* not only provides anecdotes about Wright's life, but also evaluates his works by relating them to his life and the times in which he lived, by assessing the value of his canon, by discussing and by relating the still unpublished works to the rest of the canon. Such a study as Fabre's will remain indispensable to the study of Richard Wright. And Addison Gayle's *Richard Wright: The Ordeal of a Native Son* (1980) answers many questions surrounding Wright's political activities in America and abroad. Gayle's biography appropriately supplements Wright's four sociopolitical tracts— *Black Power* (1954), *The Color Curtain* (1956), *Pagan Spain* (1956), and *White Man, Listen!* (1957), all written abroad. For Wright was as much a political activist as he was a novelist. But that is not to imply that he sacrificed art for the sake of politics or politics for art. He was concerned with the human condition and he chose diverse arenas in which to engage in the battle to improve humanity. While Gayle emphasizes the political influences on Wright's life and Fabre the literary, Margaret Walker Alexander's forthcoming *The Daemonic Genius of Richard Wright* is a psychological biography that addresses those elements of Wright's psyche which attracted him to the political, social, literary, and philosophical ideas that imbue his art.

At the end of his study, Fabre makes a final comment about Wright that seems to have escaped the perception of many scholars:

> . . . we must not forget that Richard Wright was attempting more than entertainment or even political enlightenment. Uncertainly at times, but more often quite consciously, he was grappling with a definition of man. Although his solitary quest ended prematurely and did not allow him to find one, his achievement as a writer and a humanist makes him, in the Emersonian sense, a truly "representative man" of our time. (531)

Too much of the criticism so far on *Native Son* falls short of addressing the intricacies of the human experience born out in Wright's characterization of Bigger Thomas. If Wright's portrayal of Bigger is a stage in the development of Wright's "grappling with a definition of man," categorizing *Native Son* as mainly naturalistic or existential reflects a far more pessimistic view of man than, I believe, Wright intended. In reference to a long proposed work that Wright never finished, Houston Baker explains that he interprets Wright's works as "celebrations of life, particularly the complex life lived by black Americans" (73).

Ironically, the essay from which this quotation is taken is a part of the critical mechanism responsible for the stagnation in the criticism written on Richard Wright in particular and in the literary critical network in general. Baker's comment first appears in the essay "Racial Wisdom and Richard Wright's *Native Son*," from his landmark study *Long Black Song: Essays in Black American Literature and Culture* (1972). During the same year, it was included as the introduction to Baker's edition of *Twentieth-Century Interpretations of "Native Son."* In fact, this entire collection, as is rather customary in literary criticism, reprints some of the most incisive, definitive essays on Richard Wright and *Native Son*. However, the ten years between the publication of Baker's *Long Black Song* and the collected *Twentieth-Century Interpretations of "Native Son"* and publication of Yoshinobu Hakutani's recent *Critical Essays on Richard Wright* (1982) do not bring with them a new essay on *Native Son*. All essays devoted to the novel in Hakutani's edition are reprints, including at least the third appearance of Baker's "Racial Wisdom and Richard Wright's *Native Son*."

Repetition, which is partly rooted in the human tendency to become comfortable with the familiar, seems to characterize the processes of literary criticism; but the critiques surrounding Black authors, especially Richard Wright, reflect critical and theoretical stagnation. In his provocative "Generational Shifts and the Recent Criticism of Afro-American Literature," Baker cites the late Larry Neal's succinct summation of the dilemma peculiar to the Afro-American creative artist and literary critic:

> The historical problem of black literature is that it has in a sense been perpetually hamstrung by its need to address itself to the question of racism in America. Unlike black music, it has rarely been allowed to exist on its own terms, but rather [has] been utilized as a means of public relations in the struggle for human rights. Literature can indeed make excellent propaganda, but through propaganda alone the black writer can never perform the highest function of his art: that of revealing to man his most enduring human possibilities and limitations. (10)

"Excellent propaganda" is another name for protest literature. The protest novel written by Black writers blatantly and unflinchingly condemns racism, severely rebuking its economic, sociological, and psychological effects on the lives of Black people. The history of the Black American novel directly parallels the history of the Black Americans the novels describe. From Harriet Wilson and William Wells Brown to Richard Wright and Toni Morrison, Black writers, to varying degrees and through diverse techniques, have always predominantly concerned themselves with their relation to the dominant culture. For the Black American novelist has always protested. But because of the emotional and historical side effects of racism, the mere mention of "protest literature" or provocative subject matter that highlights the lives of Blacks solicits an entire chain of programmed responses that obscures the subtleties of technique and inhibits fresh, stimulating discourse on works by Black writers. Consequently, once an idea is accepted, it becomes paradigmatic, as exemplified by the continual reprints of well-known essays on any given writer, in this instance Richard Wright.

All of the studies on *Native Son* mentioned earlier accept as a foregone conclusion that Bigger is the existential rebel thwarted because of his blackness by economic, political, and psychological forces. Katherine Fishburn, in *Richard Wright's Hero: The Faces of a Rebel-Victim*, succinctly describes the merger of naturalism and existentialism in Wright's characterization of Bigger, as her title suggests:

> Although *Native Son*, is without question, a proletarian novel, it remains something more. In this powerful novel Wright straddles the opposing forces of naturalism and existentialism, wearing the boots of a Marxist. At first Bigger Thomas seems to be at the mercy of his environment, determined by nature and society to become a killer. But Bigger, using sheer will, manages to transcend his world, to accept himself for what he is and to accept the consequences of what he has done. (71)

This view of Bigger as victim and rebel is a paradigm for what critics cite as the relationship between Wright's works and his life.

One of the most influential studies on Richard Wright, Keneth Kinnamon's *The Emergence of Richard Wright*, demonstrates this point:

> It is important to consider in some detail each of these four basic facts of Wright's youth—his racial status, his poverty, the disruption of his family, and his faulty education—not only because collectively and individually they left ineradicable scars on his psyche and deeply influenced his thought, but also because they provide much of the subject matter of his early writing. Social reality determined Wright's literary personality, even if his successful efforts to become a writer constituted a gesture of mastery over that reality. (4)

Although Kinnamon continues to belabor biographical factors as the initial determinants of the author's personality, he must be given credit for seeing literary mastery as something won through struggle. This "gesture of mastery" is what Ellison and Baldwin see as the sine qua non—that which distinguishes the artist—of the literary endeavor. Yet, by implication or neglect, literary criticism on Richard Wright so far has failed to prove that he possessed these credentials.

It was inevitable that Baldwin and Ellison—the two Black writers to follow Wright and to be most accepted by the literary mainstream—would become involved in the controversy over *Native Son* and protest fiction. Passages from their most frequently cited essays suggest at once the similarity between protest fiction and naturalism, as well as Baldwin's and Ellison's contention that these fictional modes skirt the main issue of the rendering of the writing. In his "Everybody's Protest Novel," a response to *Native Son*, Baldwin discusses what he sees as the heart of the limitations of protest fiction written by Black writers:

> . . . our humanity is our burden, our life; we need not battle for it; we need only to do what is infinitely more difficult—that is, accept it. The failure of the protest novel lies in its rejection of life, the human being, the denial of his beauty,

dread, power, in its insistence that it is his categorization alone which is real and which cannot be transcended. (17)

Whereas Baldwin is concerned with what he sees as the apologetic tendency inherent in the content of protest fiction, Ellison rejects what he sees as the banal craft of protest fiction:

> . . . protest is *not* the source of the inadequacy characteristic of most novels by Negroes, but the simple failure of craft, bad writing; the desire to have protest perform the difficult tasks of art; the belief that racial suffering, social injustice or ideologies of whatever mammy-made variety, is enough. . . . good art . . . commands attention of itself, whatever the writer's politics or point of view. . . . skill is developed by hard work, study and a conscious assault upon one's own fear and provincialism. (137)

Ellison, in contrast to Baldwin, does not condemn protest fiction for its particular portrayal of Black humanity; he instead attacks it for what he believes to be a serious imbalance between form and content, the scales weighted down heaviest on the content side.

The Ellison-Baldwin antithesis reflects the same critical skirmish, outlined earlier, which underlies what Larry Neal refers to as the "historical problem of black literature." Ellison shares with Larry Neal the idea that good art demands that there be an inextricable union between method and message. The cliché that now characterizes protest fiction and naturalism is that works written within these modes are distinguished more by social propaganda than by an interest in aesthetics. Just as it was natural for Harriet Wilson, Frances E. W. Harper, and William Wells Brown to adopt the sentimental methodology of their day to delineate the ramifications of slavery, it was equally natural for Richard Wright to choose the mode of naturalistic fiction to describe the evils of racism. Both the literature of protest and naturalistic fiction—a particular mode of protest—focus on society's mistreatment of an individual and of a particular group of individuals. When Ellison accuses many protest writers of being bad writers, he is not referring to Richard Wright. His sensitive and perceptive reading of *Native Son* in "Richard Wright's Blues" pinpoints Wright's adroit skill at transforming the personal and the environmental into art. What Ellison does highlight, though, is the inferior status given protest literature. Baldwin's denunciation of the tendency of protest literature to categorize, to deny man's beauty and power, challenges the very core of naturalism.

Essentially, as explained in Charles Child Walcutt's *American Literary Naturalism, A Divided Stream* (1956) and Donald Pizer's more recent *Twentieth-Century American Literary Naturalism: An Interpretation* (1982), the naturalistic novelist transforms Darwinian determinism into literary thought. Human beings become victims of their environment, encaged by socioeconomic forces they cannot control and driven by fundamental drives they do not understand. (As supplement to Walcutt's analysis, see Pizer 3–10. I have previously used this same definition of naturalism along with Ellison and Baldwin's attitude toward protest fiction in a discussion, similar to this one, aimed at illuminating the pitfalls of categorization in interpreting Ann Petry's novels. See Joyce, "Ann Petry" 16–20.) The idea that Bigger Thomas is a victim of his environment remains the prominent interpretation of Wright's characterization of him in *Native Son*. For Richard Wright's Marxist ideology, his Communist affiliations, his sensational subject matter, and his open explanation of the relationship between his art and the sociological and economic lives of Black people in "Blueprint for Negro Writing" have indelibly marked him as a protest writer and *Native Son* as an exemplum of naturalistic fiction. This naturalistic-existential-biographical triad subsequently results in three main levels of irony that govern the traditional view of Wright's characterization of Bigger and, simultaneously, Wright's status as an artist.

The idea that Bigger is primarily a victim of his environment strips him of the beauty and psychical mysteries that characterize the human personality. Yet, the accompanying critical attitude is that through sheer will Bigger manages, to some degree, to isolate

himself from the plight of those around him and hence transcends
environmental forces by his growth into self-knowledge. Kinnamon's statement implies that Wright, like Bigger, transcended overwhelming obstacles in achieving his success as a writer, and more
importantly that Wright, again like Bigger, was torn between the
same contradictory tensions of despair and rebellion. From this
perspective *Native Son* becomes primarily an extension of Wright's
personality. A deeper reading of the novel demands that we move
away from polemical biography.

The third level of irony emerges as the most striking. The tensions between the contradictory elements that critics see as the
components of Bigger's and Wright's personalities reflect the same
opposing elements that Charles Walcutt outlines as the embodiments of naturalism. "The elements of these contradictions, which
I have illustrated at such length, are contained in every piece of
naturalistic writing. There is always the tension between hope and
despair, between rebellion and apathy, between defying nature and
submitting to it, between celebrating man's impulses and trying to
educate them, between embracing the universe and regarding its
dark abysses with terror" (17). One a literary movement and the
other a philosophical concept, naturalism and existentialism are
contemporaneous nineteenth- and twentieth-century responses to
what men and women perceived as a hostile and an indifferent universe. Because naturalism is inherently pessimistic and existentialism optimistic, we usually do not think of them as two sides of
the same coin. Walcutt's delineation of the contradictions inherent
in naturalistic writing illuminates the underlying affinity between
the two modes of thought.

To view Bigger Thomas's characterization and the impetus behind Wright's creativity from the constructs of naturalism and
existentialism falls short of capturing not only the beauty that
Longinus refers to as the sublime, but also the subtle intricacies of
Wright's technique responsible for the power of *Native Son*. The
key to moving beyond the narrow doors of naturalism and existentialism in interpreting *Native Son* is buried in Wright's inexhaust-

ible commitment to knowledge and in our ability to penetrate the established, prejudicial critical walls that immure Bigger as primarily an environmental victim. Addressing the vision necessary for the Black writer, Wright in "Blueprint for Negro Writing" says, ". . . it should have a *complex simplicity*. Eliot, Stein, Joyce, Proust, Hemingway, and Anderson; Gorky, Barbusse, Nexo, and Jack London no less than the folklore of the Negro himself should form the heritage of the Negro writer. Every iota of grain in human thought and sensibility should be ready grist for his mill, no matter how far-fetched they may seem in their immediate implications" (44–45). This insatiable interest in human thought manifests itself in the diversity of Wright's literary technique. Robert Felgar too narrowly summarizes the multiplicity of Wright's literary method: "His literary technique is multiple: Socialist Realism, social protest, Naturalism, Gothicism, diatribe—he used any literary method he thought would work; he was no technical purist" (106). As demonstrated here, even when literary criticism does point to the diversity of Wright's technique, it fails to view his works beyond the lenses of socialism, victimization, denunciation, and the macabre, all manifestations of a pessimistic view of reality. It seems feasible, however, that an artist's craft—the shaping of his or her vision— could reflect the same kind of diversity as "every iota of grain" ground into his thought processes. And at the far extreme from this idea is the possibility that the finished product of an artistic endeavor contains elements that remained cognitive during the creative process. An interpretation of Bigger Thomas as a tragic hero lies between these two extremes.

The ideological relationship of naturalism and existentialism to tragedy is the clue which directs the way to interpreting Bigger as a tragic hero and *Native Son* as a tragedy. Explaining the interrelationship between naturalism and existentialism in Bigger's characterization, Fishburn writes:

> Bigger's success derives from an act of pure violence, another intersection of naturalism and existentialism in *Native Son*. Violence rages in many forms through most naturalistic litera-

> ture; sheer animal survival is the key activity. . . . Existen-
> tialism also explores man's capacities for violence. . . . Meta-
> physical rebellion begins with protest against man's situation.
> It leads to the deification of man; God's order is replaced by
> man's, often through violence and crime. (75)

A philosophical concept describing an individual's violent refusal
to accept the strictures and limitations of the environment, existentialism moves beyond naturalism. And tragedy extends the limits of existentialism. In the chapter on *Doctor Faustus*, Richard B.
Sewall's *A Vision of Tragedy* pinpoints violence and rebellion as
essential constituents of the tragic form:

> It is said that the great tragedies deal with the great eccen-
> trics and offenders, the God-defiers, the murderers, the adul-
> terers. But it is not tragedy's primary concern to establish the
> moral truth or the sociological meaning of the hero's action. It
> is the orthodox world, and not the tragic artist, which judges
> (or prejudges) a Job or an Oedipus, a Faustus or a Hester Prynne.
> To bring his protagonist swiftly to the point of ultimate test,
> the artist imagines a deed which violently challenges the ac-
> cepted social and (it may be) legal ways. Hence the fact that
> tragic heroes are often criminals in the eyes of society, and
> hence the frequency of the legal trial as a symbolic situation
> in tragedy from Aeschylus to Dostoevski and Kafka. (61–62)

Wright's characterization of Bigger goes beyond challenging the
"moral truth" and the "sociological meaning of the hero's action."
For Bigger's accidental murder of Mary Dalton catapults him into
the "symbolic situation" of the trial, the force which compels Bigger to come to terms with the meaning of existence.

Although violence and rebellion are indigenous to the forms of
naturalism, existentialism, and tragedy, the conclusions drawn
about the meaning of human existence mark their points of demarcation. Whereas naturalism views human beings as total victims of
their environment, existentialism argues that human existence is
unexplainable. Tragedy, on the other hand, not only finds meaning
in human existence but also celebrates it. The tragic hero, as im-

plied in a passage from T. R. Henn's *The Harvest of Tragedy*, finds redemption and meaning in the struggle to pursue freedom to the limit:

> Tragedy, even when its conclusions appear to be pessimistic, does not accept this limitation [human limitations as a norm of human conduct]. In this apparent wreckage of human aspirations which it perceives there is implicit, not only the possibility of redemption, but the spiritual assertion that man is splendid in his ashes, and can transcend his nature that Rousseau thought perfectible and that Freud once thought evil.
>
> The possibility of redemption may be perceived in many forms. If we are to use non-Christian terminology, we are confronted with the essential fact that man's desires exceed his limitations in the universe in which he is set; and that from this evil must spring. (288)

That evil springs from the very act which brings redemption forms the crux of the paradox characteristic of tragedy. The events that lead to Bigger's murder of Mary and the results of his subsequent actions illustrate that "curious blend of the inevitable and the incongruous which is peculiar to tragedy" (Frye 38).

Bigger's sense of himself—his pride—is in constant conflict with society's attitude toward him throughout the novel. After accidentally committing a murder, he is courageous enough both to accept the consequences of his actions and, for a time, to choose or control the way in which society deals with him. Bigger's success at controlling his life finds its source in Wright's beliefs in the values of this world. Instead of being primarily a novel of social protest aimed at condemning racist societal evils, *Native Son* is an affirmation of life which charts Bigger's growth into self-awareness. It is not enough that Bigger understands his world is racist; what is important is how he deals with himself in such a world. Once he resolves this dilemma, he must move on to understand his relationship to other human beings in society, both Black and white. Thus *Native Son* reflects Wright's belief that redemption for the oppressed individual—and for any individual—depends upon inner strength, that spiritual strength which makes man "splendid in his ashes" and enables him to transcend the evils of societal forces. Wright's attraction to Communism substantiated his faith in humanity, not in political institutions. This same belief in humanity caused his disillusionment with the party and his subsequent rejection of the party and its hypocrisy. More important, Wright's perception of a similar kind of insincerity spurred him to begin work on *Native Son*. In the essay "How 'Bigger' Was Born," his explanation of the impetus behind the novel illuminates the strategy which underlies his characterization of Bigger Thomas:

> The second event that spurred me to write of Bigger was more personal and subtle [the first was his work at the Southside Boys' Club in Chicago]. I had written a book of short stories which was published under the title of *Uncle Tom's Children*. When the reviews of that book began to appear, I realized that I had made an awfully naïve mistake. I found that I had written a book which even bankers' daughters could read and weep over and feel good about. I swore to myself that if I ever wrote another book, no one would weep over it; that it would be so hard and deep that they would have to face it without the consolation of tears. (xxvii)

Determined, then, to strike the appropriate balance between pity and fear, Wright, having learned of the ineffectiveness of pathos or melodrama, intended that the readers of *Native Son* achieve enough distance from Bigger to question and feel the nature of human existence.

Consequently, in the above passage, Wright evinces an awareness of the integral, interdependent relationship of form, meaning, and reader response. D. D. Raphael's essay "Why Does Tragedy Please," collected in Robert W. Corrigan's *Tragedy: Vision and Form*, parallels what Wright says about the aesthetic distance necessary to fulfill his purpose:

> Tragedy is a form of art, and its pleasure is an aesthetic pleasure. We rarely, if ever, obtain from the so-called tragedies of

life the satisfaction that we gain from tragic drama. In life, we are on the same level as those who suffer, we are fellow human beings. Our sympathy for their disaster is usually too strong for feelings of satisfaction at any sublimity they may display. In the theatre, the way is clear for the appreciation of sublimity by giving us the "God's-eye view." The scene is set in the past, so that we know what is going to happen; or, if not in the past, in the distant clime, so that we shall not be too disposed to identify ourselves in sympathy with the characters on stage. The dramatist fails in his purpose if . . . he represents life close to his audience and inhibits admiration by excessive pity. (197)

Bigger's extremely sullen personality, his ever-present potential for violence, his murder of Mary, his gory disposal of her body, and his murder of Bessie all serve as dramatic tools Wright uses to assure that his readers maintain, to use Raphael's words, a "God's-eye view" of Bigger, thus achieving an aesthetic distance that reaches deeper than pity into the caverns of human consciousness.

Raphael's summation of the aesthetic distance necessary for the tragic form evokes at once the question of the relationship of pathos or melodrama to tragedy, and the question of whether the traditional tragic form is appropriate to describe modern society. Northrop Frye's incisive definition of pathos serves as an enlightening basis for a distinction between the use of pathos in naturalism and in tragedy. Frye writes, "The root idea of pathos is the exclusion of an individual on our own level from a social group to which he is trying to belong" (39). Although Bigger is excluded from all social groups, Wright ensures that the reader does not feel excessive pity for his protagonist by characterizing him as both awful and awesome. He moves Bigger beyond the naturalistic descriptions of characters like Norris's McTeague, Crane's Maggie, and Dreiser's Clyde Griffiths. Typical of the tragic hero, Bigger has a strong sense of pride that is an integral element of his fate and thus the source of the conflict between the inevitable and the incongruous in the novel.

Moreover, a modern misconception is to associate melodrama exclusively with sentimental, propagandistic, and naturalistic literature. However, it is through the melodramatic aspects of tragedy that we experience the catharsis described originally in Aristotle's *Poetics*. Oedipus's blindness, Lear's brokenheartedness, Othello's suicide, and the numerous murders in *Macbeth* are all rooted in violent, extravagant emotions. Different from those of the sentimental literary modes, the protagonists in tragedies are never stripped of their dignity. Eric Bentley humorously and astutely captures the point of merger between the melodrama characteristic of naturalism and that of tragedy:

> Yet the idea of such a scale is misleading if it suggests that tragedy is utterly distinct from melodrama. There is a melodrama in every tragedy just as there is a child in every adult. It is not tragedy, but Naturalism, that tries to exclude childish and melodramatic elements. William Archer, a Naturalist, defined melodrama as "illogical and sometimes irrational tragedy." The premise is clear: tragedy is logical and rational. Looking for everyday logic and reasonableness in tragedy, Archer remorselessly drew the conclusion that most tragedy of the past was inferior to the middle class drawing-room drama of London around 1910. Had he been consistent he would even have included Shakespeare in the indictment.
>
> But tragedy is not melodrama minus the madness. It is melodrama plus something. (230–31)

This something which melodrama lacks emerges as part of the stimulating force behind the controversy over the nature of tragedy in the modern world.

Because tragedy traditionally recorded the lives of ruling kings and their royal families, and because Greek culture—and to some extent Renaissance culture—consisted of a societal system in which institutions, practices, and feelings were all interrelated, some early twentieth-century scholars held that traditional tragedy was not possible in the modern world (Williams 17). They believed

it was not the appropriate form to describe a society characterized by fragmentation and disillusionment. From different perspectives both Richard Sewall in *The Vision of Tragedy* and Raymond
Williams in *Modern Tragedy* trace the history of tragedy. While
Sewall focuses on the critical skirmish around the nature of tragedy, Williams emphasizes the history of the cultural changes that
underlie the tragic mode. Sewall cites the ideas of Macneile Dixon
and Joseph Wood Krutch, who saw no hope of tragedy in the modern world because contemporary society lacked cosmic order, faith
in the glory of God, and a belief in the dignity of man (128). In
tracing the ideological framework of tragedy, Williams explains
that tragedy began in a culture which emphasized "rank" and "he-
roic stature" and made no distinctions between social and metaphysical categories. According to Williams, both Renaissance and
neoclassical tragedians concern themselves with the lives of famous men (23). His discussion of the critical attitude that accompanies tragedy intersects Sewall's: "Broadly, the idea of tragedy
ceased to be metaphysical and became critical, though this development was not complete until the neoclassical critics of the
seventeenth century. . . . Over the next two centuries, until the
radical Hegelian revision, the idea of tragedy comprises mainly
methods and effects. But in fact, behind this critical emphasis,
the assumption of the nature of a tragic action was changing radi-
cally" (25).

Possibly no two works demonstrate this radical change in the
ideas concerning tragedy better than Arthur Miller's famous essay
"Tragedy and the Common Man" and Herman Melville's *Moby-
Dick*. Of course, the title of Miller's essay quite appropriately illuminates his thesis: "the common man is as apt a subject for tragedy in its highest sense as kings were" (148). He continues:

> As a general rule, to which there may be exceptions un-
> known to me, I think the tragic feeling is evoked in us when
> we are in the presence of a character who is ready to lay down
> his life, if need be, to secure one thing—his sense of personal

dignity. From Orestes to Hamlet, Medea to Macbeth, the underlying struggle is that of the individual attempting to gain his "rightful" position in his society.

Sometimes he is one who has been displaced from it, sometimes one who seeks to attain it for the first time, but the fateful wound from which the inevitable events spiral is the wound of indignity, and its dominant force is indignation. Tragedy, then, is the consequence of a man's total compulsion to evaluate himself justly. (148–49)

Miller's definition of tragedy is most notable and significant for its discounting of the class distinction associated with tragedy.

In Chapter 26 of *Moby-Dick* ("Knights and Squires"), Melville, focusing on this same idea of dignity, has much earlier elevated the stature of the common man to that of the tragic hero. An embodiment of the theme of democratic dignity, Melville's tragic hero is the common man who struggles to realize the ideal within himself. In what is stylistically a sort of incantation to his muse, Melville has Ishmael say:

But this august dignity I treat of, is not the dignity of kings and robes, but that abounding dignity which has no robed investiture. Thou shalt see it shining in the arm that wields a pick or drives a spike; that democratic dignity which, on all hands, radiates without end from God; Himself! The great God absolute! . . .

If, then, to meanest mariners, and renegades and castaways, I shall hereafter ascribe high qualities, though dark; weave round them tragic graces; if even the most mournful, perchance the most abased, among them all, shall at times lift himself to the exalted mounts; . . . then against all mortal critics bear me out in it, thou just Spirit of Equality, which hast spread one royal mantle of humanity over all my kind! Bear me out in it, thou great democratic God! . . . Thou who didst pick up Andrew Jackson from the pebbles; who didst hurl him upon a warhorse; who didst thunder him higher than a throne! Thou who, in all Thy mighty earthly march-

ings, ever cullest Thy selectest champions from the kingly
commons; bear me out in it, O God! (160–61)

Melville's Ahab and Miller's Willie Loman join a long list of tragic
heroes whose idealized aspirations far exceed their human limitations. Consequently, from the fourth century B.C., with the appearance of Aristotle's *Poetics*, to the 1949 publication of Miller's
"Tragedy and the Common Man," the concept of tragedy under-
went a notable change reflective of the societal values of various
epochs.

The underlying consistency in the characterization of the tragic
hero—whether a king or common person—is the dignity that
motivates the hero and isolates him psychologically and many
times physically from the rest of society. Thus dignity, an important embodiment of the tragic character's personality, elicits the
reader's admiration of the spiritual strength peculiar to the tragic
hero despite the hero's socioeconomic status. Moreover, achieving
a synthesis between form and meaning, traditional tragedies required a highly stylized form to describe their noble protagonists.
The above passage from Melville exemplifies the elevated language
he uses elsewhere in his descriptions of Ahab. Hence the language
used in the exploration of the tragic theme parallels the tragic
writer's perception of the hero, becoming an integral part of the
process which distinguishes the tragic hero from all other characters. The stylized language of tragedy separates it, to some extent,
from naturalistic expression. While Crane strips language to its
bare essentials in *Maggie*, Dreiser in *An American Tragedy* chooses
to tell his story through an omniscient narrator skilled in the art
of reportage. Naturalistic literature, in other words, does not use
language to celebrate life or to aggrandize its hero. The reason for
this is clear: naturalism sees little to celebrate; essentially, its purpose is to condemn.

An effective means of encapsulating the distinctions made so far
in this introduction between naturalism and tragedy, and of outlin-
ing the strategy I shall use in the chapters to follow, is to juxtapose
briefly Dreiser's characterization of Clyde Griffiths—a quintes-

sential naturalistic protagonist—to Wright's portrayal of Bigger
Thomas. For the Robert Nixon trial and Dreiser's *An American
Tragedy* are structural influences on *Native Son*. Although both
Dreiser and Wright depict their protagonists as products of American society and share the idea that society is in part to blame for
their crimes, Wright breaks two of the salient rules of naturalism
when he has Bigger control his situation by manipulating the environment that seeks to victimize him. Clyde Griffiths, on the
other hand, remains a total victim. Moreover, the most important
difference in the portrayals of these two young men is Bigger's spiritual growth or transcendence. Unlike Clyde, Bigger learns intensely
from his experiences. He discovers himself, recognizing who he is
and what has caused his fall. Clyde is "motionless in time." He is
basically as dimly aware of the forces that motivate him at the end
of the novel as he is at the beginning. While Dreiser highlights the
cause of Clyde's crime, Wright focuses on the result of Bigger's
murder of Mary (Hakutani 168, 171). Therefore, if we see Bigger's
murder of Mary as the beginning of his journey into self-discovery,
it is easy to shift our focus from Wright's condemnation of societal
evils to his affirmation of Bigger's willingness to lay down his life
to obtain his sense of personal dignity.

My analysis of *Native Son* as a tragedy and of Bigger Thomas as
a tragic character does not at all mean I am suggesting that tragedy
and didacticism or condemnation are antithetical. The fact is that
tragedy, too, contains an essential element of the reprehensible. In
describing the tragic vision, Sewall pinpoints the goal of tragedy as
challenging human nature and rebuking passivity:

> Nor is the tragic vision for those who, though admitting
> unsolved questions and the reality of guilt, anxiety, and suffer-
> ing, would become quietist and do nothing. Mere sensitivity
> is not enough. The tragic vision impels the man of action to
> fight against his destiny, kick against the pricks, and state his
> case before God or his fellows. . . . The writing of tragedy is
> the artist's way of taking action, of defying destiny, and this is

why in the great tragedies there is a sense of the artist's own involvement, an immediacy not so true of the forms, like satire and comedy, where the artist's position seems more detached. (5)

Hence the act of writing tragedy and the nature of tragedy to strip the tragic hero of all worldly dependencies involve the tragedian in the struggle for the improvement of human kind. A prolific reader and subtle thinker, Wright was too skillful an artist and too astute a political activist to jeopardize his literary aspirations by overemphasizing propaganda at the expense of the sublimity which underlies great works of literature.

Finally, the most telling distinction between protest literature and the sublimity of tragedy is that protest literature easily becomes dated while tragedy, striking at the core of what it means to be a human being, remains perpetually powerful. The 200,000 copies of *Native Son* that sold during its first month of publication attest to its power. Its having been translated into seventeen foreign languages and its secure position in many curricula in American literature reaffirm its power. The source of this impact is not Bigger's murder of a white woman or his sensational disposal of her remains. The intensity of the novel comes from Wright's masterful handling of language, the adroit synthesis he achieves between his message and the form that shapes the message. The entire linguistic network of the novel hinges on a complex system of ironies that metaphorically parallels the inevitability and incongruity of the elements that make up Bigger's life. When he describes the rhythms of Bigger's life early in Book 1, Wright also foreshadows the intricate web of ironies that characterize his use of language: "These were the rhythms of his [Bigger's] life: indifference and violence; periods of abstract brooding and periods of intense desire; moments of silence and moments of anger—like water ebbing and flowing from the tug of a far-away, invisible force" (24–25). This description of the paradoxical nature of Bigger's personality echoes T. R. Henn's summation of the movement of the tragic form:

> Alone of all artistic forms tragedy offers no apologies for
> its incidental didacticism. . . . Its didacticism may be, and
> often is, multiform, disguised, working by paradox or antithe-
> sis, implicit in its images. In the revelation and interaction
> of character we are confronted continuously with values,
> whether implicit or explicit, stated or inferred, that are stead-
> ily related to a traditional or evolving ethic. (286)

Irreconcilable opposites characterize the tragic mode. The tragic
hero, like Bigger as Wright depicts him in the above passage, is a
divided human being who must confront conflicts that are ra-
tionally insoluble as well as obligations and passions. He must
make choices, whether for good or evil. And he errs knowingly or
involuntarily, accepts consequences, and grows into a deeper awareness of himself. He must suffer or die with his new perception of
life (Heilman, "Tragedy and Melodrama" 248). Bigger Thomas is
such a character. His realization that he is different from other human beings, but that the well-being of his family is affected by his
actions, parallels the tightly wrought ironies that unite Wright's
characterization of Bigger with a unique web of metaphor which
reflects a soul divided against itself.

In order to comprehend the full significance of the paradoxes
that underlie Wright's description of Bigger's personality, we must
first understand the influence of the environment on Bigger's perception of life. The purpose of Chapter 2 in this study is to show
that Wright exceeds the limits of naturalism in his use of setting
to represent a state of mind. He elevates the powerful environmental forces that control Bigger's life to the level of gods, much like
those who manipulate Oedipus's fate. Bigger's fate, then, is preordained by the cosmology of an environmental system which divides human beings into subgroups of Blacks and whites or into
the oppressed and the oppressors. Native Son charts what inevitably happens when these two worlds or subgroups collide.

Although Bigger responds as expected (as it is preordained) when
he encounters the powerful forces from the white environment, he
ceases to become a total victim; he chooses through sheer will and

indignation to take control of his own life, to *act* by challenging the established order of his environment. Chapter 3 demonstrates that Bigger is motivated by the same sense of pride described as *hubris* by Aristotle and Renaissance tragedians and as dignity by Arthur Miller and Herman Melville. His *hamartia* is his loss of control, his easily excited temperament. As the title of Book 1 suggests, fear is a controlling factor in Bigger's personality. Nonetheless, his accidental murder of Mary gives him a new perception of himself and of his place in society, and enables him to conquer the fear and to control his own life. His loss of control precipitates the discovery of Mary's bones and points to him as her murderer. Traditional readings of the novel stop at describing Bigger as the existential human being isolated from both the Black and white worlds because of his rebelliousness.

The view of Bigger as a tragic protagonist probes further into the intricacies of Wright's method by emphasizing the irreconcilable aspects of Bigger's personality and of his relationship to the other characters. The same Bigger who intensely fears whites—and thus appears submissive and pusillanimous—is by comparison to the other Black characters quite courageous and intractable. Unlike them, he is a man of action who "fights against his destiny" by challenging established order. Wright ensures the reader's identification with Bigger's personality through his skillful use of a third-person limited point of view. This center of consciousness—without our always being aware of it—manipulates an ironic balance between the awesome and the awful in Bigger's characterization. Because of this narrator, at no point in the novel do we cease to empathize with Bigger and to understand the psychological forces that motivate him.

Some of the intensity in the novel emerges from the tension between Bigger's hate and shame as well as between his rebelliousness and fear, while the beauty comes from the paradoxical nature of the metaphorical functions of the wall, the color yellow, the sun, the snow, the colors black and white, and the concept of blindness. Chapter 4, entitled "Technique: The Figurative Web," explores the ironies and relationships which embody the salient metaphors and images in the novel. These figurative elements illuminate the divided aspects of Bigger's character. For instance, the wall at once represents the emotional barrier Bigger keeps between himself and the world as well as the network of economic and political barriers that excite his indignation. The snow, a symbol both of Bigger's violent nature and of the sterility and insensitivity which characterize the white world that seeks to control him, merges with or parallels the paradoxical function of the wall and the metaphor of blindness. The rhythmic repetition of the metaphors of the snow, the sun and its accompanying color yellow, and the colors black and white impresses a stylized form upon the novel characteristic of the elevated language of tragedy. Another prominent aspect of this stylized form is the rhythmic repetition of the periodic, balanced, and compound sentences to depict the continual, abrupt changes in Bigger's reactions to the established order of his environment. The variation in sentence patterns to portray the movement of Bigger's thoughts corresponds to the semantic function of the metaphors used to highlight the contradictions that make up Bigger's character.

The minute aspects of language in *Native Son* form an intricate net of skillfully woven linguistic threads that become manifestations of Bigger's consciousness and thus of the themes in the novel. Though Wright successfully elevates his language to reflect Bigger's dignity, at the same time he strikes an impressive balance between Bigger's personality and the language used to describe that personality. This balance, as stated by Elder Olson in his essay "Modern Drama and Tragedy," is an integral element of tragedy: "Tragedy demands a high style, certainly; but the true high style, is simply that which is appropriate to the tragic character—one, that is, which manifests his dignity. It is not bombast. The most affecting passages in the mature Shakespeare are composed in extremely simple language, elevated only by what they manifest to us" (183).

Max's address in Book 3 further demonstrates how Wright skill-fully achieves a balance between language and meaning. The length and esoteric nature of Max's speech to the judge have drawn more negative criticism than any other aspect of *Native Son*. Chapter 5 of this study, entitled "The Unity of Book 3: A Synthesis of the Theme," will show that Max's speech is an embodiment of the dominant image patterns that depict Bigger's tragic dilemma. With Max's speech serving as the focal point, Book 3 emerges as the cli-max of Bigger's suffering through its portrayal of the relationship between Bigger and Max. Illuminating Max's failure to perceive Bigger's humanity, the speech proves to be a dramatization of Max's character. That the speech unites all the dominant image patterns that depict Bigger's humanity reflects the irony characteristic of tragedy.

In the same way that traditional readings of Bigger as a natu-ralistic and existential character and of Max's speech as gratuitous diatribe have impeded fresh insights into *Native Son*, numerous misconceptions also haunt Wright's other novels. For the idea that Wright's creativity resulted primarily from his experiences in Mis-sissippi and the implication that his political ideology was more important to him than the "sedentary toil" which, so Yeats main-tained, must go into great works, have become serious impedi-ments to new, discerning studies of his works. These prejudicial, biographical barriers must be broken down in much the same way as the territorial barriers that exclusively categorize the elements of tragedy and naturalism. For great works of art are like prisms, with diverse spectrums of life emanating from the consciousness of the creative artist. And as illustrated by our dreams, human con-sciousness is characterized by fluidity and boundlessness. Richard Wright's creative aspirations were equally boundless. As suggested by Michel Fabre, Wright's works demonstrate a quest for the mean-ing of life. The elements of this quest assume shapes as diverse as the characters in Wright's fiction. All five of his novels—*Native Son*, *The Outsider*, *Savage Holiday*, *The Long Dream*, and *Lawd*

Today—reveal that Wright was a realist. He began by accepting the reality of racism in human consciousness.

Before individuals can begin to eradicate the emotional and physical abuses of racism from their lives, they must first understand the nature of racism. From this perspective, Wright celebrates Bigger's coming into an awareness of his internalization of racist concepts. Consequently, a coming to terms with the meaning of life in *Native Son* does not demand that we attack societal evils, but that we question the manner in which we choose to deal with these evils. *Native Son* treats the essential question of the meaning of existence to a young, prideful Black man who resists the strictures of established order and chooses to act, subsequently discovering a spiritual fortitude which brings self-knowledge and a kind of prudence that approaches wisdom.

2. Setting and Structure: The Cosmology of Bigger's World

In its narrowest sense, setting refers merely to place and time of action. In *Native Son*, however, Wright adroitly uses setting in a significantly larger sense so that it becomes the "background, the social environment, the atmosphere of [the] literary work; the interrelationship of place and time to the achievement of the total work" (Hancock 24). Specifically, setting in *Native Son* depicts a physical world in which being Black means living in an impoverished milieu governed by the social and political laws of whites—laws that are manifest physically in the arrangement of entirely segregated communities—and being white means unwittingly suffering from the moral deprivation in enforcing that segregation. In "Richard Wright: Aspects of His Afro-American Literary Relations," Donald Gibson captures the essence of Wright's depiction of setting to manifest the powerful environmental forces that attempt complete control over Bigger Thomas's life. He also captures Wright's concurrent use of setting to represent his characters' states of mind. Using the title of Paul Laurence Dunbar's novel *The Sport of the Gods* as his reference point, Gibson says:

> Dunbar's characters, in his only novel that bears on this subject directly [the subject of the Black characters' relationship to their environment] are unable to do anything about their lives. For that reason he entitled this novel, which deals with Southern rural and Northern urban existence of Black people, *The Sport of the Gods*. If "we are to the gods as flies to wanton boys," then we have very little power and are in

fact simply victims of powerful, capricious forces. ("Richard Wright" 86)

In *Native Son* Richard Wright elevates the social, economic, and political components of the white world to the level of gods, doing more than depicting these environmental constituents from a merely naturalistic perspective.

Setting in *Native Son* reveals those environmental forces that make up Bigger's universe. The world described in the novel is divided into two major subgroups—one Black and the other white. The white world has complete dominance over the Black. And the moral, social, economic, and political laws which govern the individuals in these two worlds are codified by the white world and transmitted to the Black more through physical or social interaction than through any set of written codes. While the system of slavery represents the most extreme division of American society into two basic subgroups, racism, its replacement, transforms the discriminatory practices of the eighteenth and nineteenth centuries into the cosmological order of segregation. The essence of *Native Son* is that social, economic, and political practices of segregation foster demeaning, destructive psychological attitudes that imbue the personalities of both Wright's Black and white characters. Bigger's extreme fear and rebelliousness are rooted in his emotional reaction to whites and their environment, and in the white characters' superficial, programmed responses to and stereotypical expectations of him. Bigger's fear and the white characters' superciliousness stem from the all-encompassing, overwhelming power that whites have over Blacks in *Native Son*. This power manifests the same effects and controls which describe the Greeks' attitudes toward the gods and Job's toward Jehovah.

For Bigger, like Job, challenges the established world view that dictates what should be the nature of his relationship to his immediate environment and to that outside the Black community. And, as with Oedipus, the very act which he hopes will counteract his fate (his carrying Mary Dalton to her room in order to protect his job) paradoxically becomes the incident that catapults him further toward his fate. Wright's use of setting to instigate action satisfies part of Aristotle's criteria for the arousal of pity and fear. Aristotle says:

> Now it is possible for pity and fear to be aroused (1) through pageant and spectacle as well as (2) from the arrangement of the incidents. The latter is better, and is characteristic of the better poet; for the plot should be so constructed that, apart from what is taken in through the eye, anyone just listening to the incidents, as they take place, would chill with fear and thrill with pity from what is happening. (26)

To replace Aristotle's suggestion of pageant and spectacle with setting does not require too much of an imaginative leap. The descriptions of the Black community, Bigger's home, the street where he meets his friends, the movie, the white community, the Daltons' home, and the courtroom conjoin as pageant and spectacle, representing the environmental order that excites Bigger's indignation. If we are to understand the incidents as they take place without the assistance of the eye (as Aristotle proposes), then the background against which the incidents occur and which instigates the action must be assumed within the elements through which the plot unfolds. An ironic title, an epigraph from the Book of Job, and the titles of the three books in the novel are all dramatic devices which accompany setting to describe the world of *Native Son*.

Possibly no other author better expresses how the interactions between Blacks and whites in a racist society exemplify ritualistic patterns reflective of that society's world view than Ralph Ellison. His explanation of how myth and ritual in *Invisible Man* become a part of the creative process enriches our understanding of the irony in the title *Native Son* and of Wright's use of setting to accentuate his characters' behavioral patterns:

> It took me a long time to learn how to adapt such examples [themes, symbols, and usages based on folk material] of myth into my work—also ritual. The use of ritual is equally a vital

part of the creative process. I learned a few things from Eliot, Joyce and Hemingway, but not how to adapt them. When I started writing, I knew that in both *The Waste Land* and *Ulysses* ancient myth and ritual were used to give form and significance to the material; but it took me a few years to realize that the myths and rites which we find functioning in our everyday lives could be used in the same way. . . .

I don't know whether I'm getting this over or not. Let's put it this way: Take the "Battle Royal" passage in my novel, where the boys are blindfolded and forced to fight each other for the amusement of the white observers. This is a vital part of behavior pattern in the South, which both Negroes and whites thoughtlessly accept. It is a ritual in preservation of caste lines, a keeping of taboo to *appease the gods* and ward off bad luck. (173–74, emphasis mine)

Ellison here suggests that racism is such an integral element of American society that it fosters a set of habitual responses ingrained in the social network that governs interaction between Blacks and whites (Gibson 87). Understanding the role that he must play in the presence of whites, Bigger Thomas participates in the ritual of appeasing the gods. When he carries Mary Dalton in his arms up the stairs to her room, "bad luck" befalls him because he has violated the social taboo that governs their interaction.

The crux of Wright's message and its exploration is embodied in the ironic outcome of Bigger's attempt to escape his fate when he carries Mary to her room. Moreover, Bigger's entire personality embodies ironic or contradictory elements. Though his personality conforms to the strictures of the white world, environmental oppression is paradoxically responsible for his rebelliousness, which defies physical and emotional confinement. Consequently, the entire novel progresses through an unraveling of ironies and contradictions that is reflected in the unfolding of the plot, in the language of the novel, and in Bigger's consciousness. The irony begins with the title of the novel, which underlines what Ellison refers to as the ritualistic social forms that deny Bigger the right to enjoy the fruits of his American heritage. The white world view forbids

Bigger, a "native son," to expand beyond the social, economic, and political limits of his Black community. Reinforcing this idea, Carl Milton Hughes suggests that irony is the controlling device out of which the story unfolds:

> The title *Native Son* suggests ironically the contents, and this means, in context of American society, that a member by right of birth is a citizen of the country enjoying all the rights and privileges which go along with citizenship. As the story unfolds, the venomous irony and frustrating paradox in the title become unmistakably clear. (50–51)

Two key points in Hughes's explanation of the irony suggested in the title are his curious uses of the phrases "venomous irony" and "frustrating paradox." What Hughes refers to here unearths a deeper level of irony. For the same environmental restrictions of racism aimed at stifling Bigger's humanity are, in turn, responsible for the violence which leads to his fortuitous discovery of that humanity.

Trapped in Mary Dalton's room, Bigger reacts with extreme fear because he intuitively and instinctively understands that the American cosmos dictates that his life be taken if he goes beyond the limits of the taboos which restrict the interaction between Black men and white women. But once having transgressed forbidden territory, he challenges the expectation of the gods by remaining in the Daltons' home, writing the kidnap note, and framing Jan. Like Job, Bigger chooses not just to endure the test of his calamities, but to defy them. In the epigraph from the Book of Job which introduces *Native Son*, Wright proposes the affinity between the established order of Bigger's world and Job's and between their responses to the trials of their respective gods:

> Even today is my complaint rebellious,
> My stroke is heavier than my groaning. (iii)

This epigraph complements the irony reflected in the title of the novel through its suggestion of the kinship between Job's and Bigger's defiance and of the gods responsible for Bigger's and Job's complaints. Linda Hamalian's incisive summation of Wright's use of epigraphs in *The Long Dream* highlights the effect of Wright's reference to Job:

> As in the highly allusive poetry of T. S. Eliot, the epigraph cannot be ignored in Wright: though it is not an essential part of the narrative, it conveys hints of the significance or even the genesis of the work. Sometimes the epigraph will epitomize the emotional climate of the novel and sometimes the epigraph will suggest the direction that Wright's thought is taking, especially in those novels . . . in which the coherence breaks down and the plot itself does not adequately indicate Wright's intention. Together, with the title, the epigraph prepares the reader for the experience of the book. It is like the leitmotif of a symphony or the prelude to a piece of operatic music. (120)

The epigraph to *Native Son*, along with the title, does indeed give hints as to the genesis of the novel and its emotional climate. Serving as prelude, the quotation from the Book of Job makes evident that Bigger is far more than a victim of his environment and that Wright elevates the environmental forces in his novel to a level comparable to those that characterize Job's world.

Structurally, the title and the epigraph function as leitmotifs—to use Hamalian's term—that join setting in their illumination of the order inherent in Bigger's social environment. The epigraph also shows how Wright reveals character through the elements of setting. In addition to evoking the psychological and social limitations of a segregated society, the epigraph proposes that there is justice in Bigger's complaint—just as there is justice in Job's. Job's punishment is far more severe than his fault deserves (Layman's Parallel Bible 1281). Analogously, Bigger, a "native son" of America, does not deserve the alienation and maltreatment bestowed upon him by a caste society. If the reader internalizes the bitterness that Bigger feels and understands the motivations behind Bigger's violence, he or she will identify with him and possibly be saved by Bigger. Sewall cites this contradiction between the pride that motivates Bigger and Job and its accompanying negative dynamics as salient to tragedy:

> According to the Poet [author of the Book of Job], and to the Greek tragedians, pride like Job's is justified. It has its ugly and dark side, but it was through pride that Job made his spiritual gains and got a hearing from Jehovah himself. . . . The pride that moved Job is the dynamic of a whole line of tragic heroes, from Oedipus to Ahab. It is always ambiguous and often destructive, but it is the very hallmark of the type. (22)

So that he can depict the range and depth of the contradictions inherent in Bigger's personality, Wright appropriately begins Book 1 in Bigger's home.

Although "Fear," the title of Book 1, does represent Bigger's overwhelming response to his environment, it also functions as a metaphor for the collective elements of the setting or background which induces Bigger's emotional and physical reactions. The strength of Wright's descriptions of setting in Book 1 strongly affects our acceptance of Bigger's change at the end of the novel. The purpose of this first book is to introduce the environmental forces that have already shaped Bigger's life when the novel opens. We do not see Bigger's early flirtations with crime. Yet, through Wright's use of setting and its effect on Bigger's consciousness, we understand that Bigger's stifling daily routine and that of the rest of the Black Belt results from a mechanized, systematic environment with a sharp dichotomy between the rights of Blacks and those of whites. The metaphor comparing the power that whites have over Blacks to the heavens and the elements of nature suggests that setting is a great force equivalent to the power of gods:

> To Bigger and his kind white people were not really people; they were a sort of great natural force, like a stormy sky looming overhead, or like a deep swirling river stretching suddenly at one's feet in the dark. As long as he and his black folks did not go beyond certain limits, there was no need to fear that white force. But whether they feared it or not, each

and every day of their lives they lived with it; even when
words did not sound its name, they acknowledged its reality.
As long as they lived here in this prescribed corner of the city,
they paid mute tribute to it. (97)

Wright's reference to the omnipotence of whites and their omni-
presence in the consciousness of his Black characters parallels
Ellison's discussion of the ritualistic social patterns that have
shaped Black and white consciousnesses and that govern the interaction between Blacks and whites. Bigger's home is a microcosm
for the stifling emotional and physical entrapments of his "prescribed corner of the city."

Bigger, however, psychologically rebels against paying tribute to
a rat-infested, one-room, shabby apartment with "no rug on the
floor and the plastering on the walls and ceiling hung loose in
many places. There were two worn iron beds, four chairs, an old
dresser, and a drop-leaf table on which they ate" (89). Wright has
Bigger's family illustrate the emotional pestilence their small world
breeds. Bigger and his younger brother Buddy's daily ritual of clos-
ing their eyes or turning their heads so that their mother and sister
can dress is as emotionally devastating as the bloody battle between Bigger and the huge rat. Such actions are direct reflections of
living quarters which hamper self-esteem and militate against human dignity. This description of Bigger's home sharply contrasts
with that of the Daltons and enriches the irony in Max's revealing
to the judge that Mr. Dalton, Mary's father, owns the apartment
building in which Bigger lives. Mr. Dalton, then, is one of the gods
that dictate Bigger's fate by prescribing both where and how Bigger
lives. The world outside Bigger's home is as confining as that inside. When outside, he finds his choices of how to spend his time
before accepting the job at the Daltons' very limited: "He tried to
decide if he wanted to buy a ten-cent magazine, or go to a movie,
or go to the poolroom and talk with the gang, or just loaf around.
With his hands deep in his pockets, another cigarette slanting
across chin, he brooded and watched the men at work across the
street" (11). This description of Bigger reveals a young man whose

life is aimless and frustrated by the refusal of the white power-structure to permit him to function in a world larger than that of the Black Belt in which he lives. Bigger and his friends evince their disgust at the prohibitions that the white world dictates by raiding newsstands, fruitstands, and apartments. Of course, an essential part of Wright's message in *Native Son*, as exemplified by the ironic title, is the idea that Bigger, through his constant preoccupation with the comforts of the white world, has internalized the values of that world and understands that he too should be able to share in the economic and social rewards of his American heritage.

Nothing demonstrates Bigger's comprehension of the powerful forces of the white world better than the conversation in the street between him and Gus and the game of being white that they play. This entire scene sharply amplifies the elements of the setting which shape Bigger's thoughts and thus underlie his actions in the Daltons' home. While watching an airplane fly overhead, Bigger and Gus outline an economic, social, and political system similar to feudalism, characterized by housing and job discrimination, negligent landlords, a Jim Crow army, and schools of aviation that discriminate against Blacks. Preoccupied with these thoughts, Bigger coerces Gus into a "game of play-acting in which he and his friends imitate the ways and manners of white folks" (18):

> Bigger saw Gus cup his left hand in his ear, as though holding a telephone receiver; and cup his right hand to his mouth, as though talking into a transmitter.
>
> "Hello," Gus said.
>
> "Hello," Bigger said. "Who's this?"
>
> "This is Mr. J. P. Morgan speaking," Gus said.
>
> "Yessuh, Mr. Morgan," Bigger said; his eyes filled with much adulation and respect.
>
> "I want you to sell twenty thousand shares of U.S. Steel in the market this morning," Gus said.
>
> "At what price, suh?" Bigger asked.
>
> "Aw, just dump 'em at any price," Gus said with casual irritation. "We're holding too much."
>
> "Yessuh," Bigger said.

> "And call me at my club at two this afternoon and tell me if the President telephoned," Gus said. . . .
>
> "Hello," Gus answered. "Who's this?"
>
> "This is the President of the United States speaking," Bigger said. . . .
>
> "I'm calling a cabinet meeting this afternoon at four o'clock and you, as Secretary of State, *must* be there."
>
> "Well, now Mr. President," Gus said, "I'm pretty busy. They raising sand over there in Germany and I got to send 'em a note. . . ."
>
> "But this is important," Bigger said.
>
> "What you going to take up at this cabinet meeting?" Gus asked.
>
> "Well, you see, the niggers is raising sand all over the country. . . . We've got to do something with these black folks. . . ."
>
> "Oh, if it's about the niggers, I'll be right there, Mr. President," Gus said. (16–17)

From the distant perspective of their environment, Bigger and Gus evince their knowledge of the power structure and concerns of the white establishment, as well as their place within that structure.

Because Bigger knows the white world only vicariously and because Mary Dalton has an idealized, romantic concept of what it means to be Black, the conflicting psychological and environmental elements of their pasts have preordained that violence, or at best discord, be the result of their interaction. From the beginning of Book 1, Wright interweaves into the fabric of the narrative rhythmic threads that function as foreshadowing devices, which signal the approach of Bigger's fate. (In his *The Emergence of Richard Wright* [127], Kinnamon discusses the foreshadowing of subsequent events as a device that creates a sense of fate.) While the setting in Book 1 represents the established order of a Jim Crow society which shapes Bigger's consciousness and against which he rebels, "Fate," the title of Book 3, suggests the natural unfolding of the oracle of Book 1, which forewarned of Bigger's destiny. Bigger's own premonitions, his mother's warning, and Buckley's campaign poster emerge as the prominent chords sounding Bigger's outcome.

Quite early in Book 1, Bigger's mother responds to his antagonistic personality and his insolence after he dangles the dead rat in Vera's face: "And mark my word, some of these days you going to set down and *cry.* Some of these days you going to wish you made something out of yourself, instead of just a tramp. But it'll be too late then" (8). Bigger, too, feels that something sinister awaits him. When he and Gus finish their game of playing white, Bigger feels his intense indignation at a Jim Crow society:

> "Naw. But I just can't get used to it," [to Jim Crow laws and not being able to do the things he wishes] Bigger said. "I swear to God I can't. I know I oughtn't think about it, but I can't help it. Every time I think about it I feel like somebody's poking a red-hot iron down my throat. Goddammit, look! We live here and they live there. We black and they white. They got things and we ain't. They do things and we can't. It's just like living in jail. Half the time I feel like I'm on the outside of the world peeping in through a knot-hole in the fence. . . ."
> . . . "Sometimes I feel like something awful's going to happen to me," Bigger spoke with a tinge of bitter pride in his voice. (17)

Throughout Book 1, Wright sharply juxtaposes Bigger's "bitter pride" against the background of environmental, omnipotent forces that try to dictate where he lives, how he lives, what he owns, and what he thinks of himself. Buckley, the district attorney, emerges in Book 3 as the perfect representative of the white world that seeks to destroy Bigger. As part of the foreshadowing of Bigger's destiny, Buckley first appears in Book 1. The language that describes him evokes the mystery and fear induced by the elements that make up setting. As Bigger watches the workmen hang a poster of Buckley to a signboard, the narrator explains:

> When the men were through they gathered up their pails and brushes and got into the truck and drove off. He looked at the poster: the white face was fleshy but stern; one hand was uplifted and its index finger pointed straight out into the street at each passer-by. The poster showed one of those faces that

> looked straight at you when you looked at it and all the while
> you were walking and turning your head to look at it it kept
> looking unblinkingly back at you until you got so far from it
> you had to take your eyes away, and then it stopped, like a
> movie blackout. Above the top of the poster were tall red
> letters: IF YOU BREAK THE LAW, YOU CAN'T WIN! (11)

This poster, which is part of Buckley's campaign for reelection as
district attorney, is conspicuous both because of the suggestion of
his personality deduced from the look on his face and because
Buckley has it placed in the heart of the Black community. For the
message at the end is aimed at warning the Black community of
the firm hand of the law and simultaneously soliciting that community's vote. Full of the control and self-confidence implied by
his description on the poster, Buckley symbolizes the power of a
world that Bigger understands only abstractly.

Bigger's preoccupation with and fear of the white world, his
vague understanding of its social network, and his premonition
that something destructive will happen to him all coalesce as elements of the foreshadowing which conform to what Karl Jaspers
describes as the "tragic atmosphere": "The tragic atmosphere arises
as the strange and sinister fate to which we have been abandoned.
There is something alien that threatens us, something we cannot
escape. Wherever we go, whatever we see, whatever we hear, there
is something in the air which will destroy us, no matter what we
do or wish" (45). Bigger gets closer to his "strange and sinister fate"
as soon as he enters the white community en route to the Daltons'
home. The spaciousness of the white neighborhood sharply contrasts with the stultifying conditions of his Southside community.
From the moment he enters Mary Dalton's world, he feels threatened and uneasy. The narrator describes Bigger's discomfort with
this alien world as he sits waiting for Mr. Dalton:

> He felt that the position in which he was sitting was too awk-
> ward and found that he was on the very edge of the chair. He
> rose slightly to sit farther back; but when he sat he sank
> down so suddenly and deeply that he thought the chair had

collapsed under him. . . . He looked round the room; it was lit by dim lights glowing from a hidden source. . . . He had not expected anything like this; he had not thought that this world would be so utterly different from his own that it would intimidate him. . . . He was sitting in a white home; dim lights burned round him; strange objects challenged him; and he was feeling angry and uncomfortable. (39)

Wright is meticulous in his representation of the differences between Bigger's and Mary's homes, as well as their social and economic backgrounds. He uses setting to demonstrate that the environmental forces and their accompanying emotional counterparts create a chasm between Blacks and whites so destructive that it makes both races alien to the humanity of the other.

The conversation between Mr. and Mrs. Dalton in Bigger's presence characterizes them as representatives of the powerful alien world that governs Bigger's life. After Bigger responds to Mrs. Dalton's question about his educational level, she addresses her husband as if Bigger has disappeared: "Don't you think it would be a wise procedure to inject him into his new environment at once, so he could get the feel of things?" (40). The language here is much like that of the doctors in the hospital in Ellison's *Invisible Man* (1953). Ellison's point echoes Wright's—the language used by these representatives of the white world illuminates the power and aloofness that underlie their involvement with those whose lives they seek to control. Bigger's thoughts in response to this alien language imply the exalted, unearthly status he attributes to the Daltons:

Bigger listened, blinking and bewildered. The long strange words they used made no sense to him; it was another language. He felt from the tone of their voices that they were having a difference of opinion about him, but he could not determine what it was about. It made him uneasy, tense, as though there were influences and presences about him which he could feel but not see. (40)

The epitome of her parents' world view, Mary Dalton emerges as the goddess who concretizes Bigger's fear and uneasiness.

Just as the constituents of the setting illustrate the causes of Bigger's fearful, stunted, rebellious character, the vastness and looseness of Drexel Boulevard and Mary Dalton's home reflect her irrepressible and irresponsible personality. Upon first meeting Bigger, she completely fails to see how her mentioning of unions and capitalists and her carefree, intimate manner frighten Bigger and make him uncomfortable. She is unable to identify with his human perceptions. Like her parents, she views him as an object. Romantic, myopic liberals, Mary and Jan do not understand how the difference between their skin color and Bigger's has fostered deep, emotional differences between their and his response to the world. They do not understand why Bigger is so adamantly against eating with them in Ernie's Kitchen Shack. The narrator succinctly captures the social dividing line that separates Mary and Jan's world from Bigger's, accentuating setting to represent the godlike status of whites and their power: "The people in Ernie's Kitchen Shack knew him and he did not want them to see him with these white people. He knew that if he went in they would ask one another: *Who're them white folks Bigger's hanging around with!*" (61). Wright's emphasis indicates the impact of the word *white* or any reference to white people on the minds of Blacks. Embodied in the phrase *white folks* are over three hundred years of intuitive cultural associations. These associations make up what Ellison refers to as the ritualistic social forms that characterize a Jim Crow society. Wright demonstrates how Blacks and whites pay tribute to these rituals and illustrates what happens when any member of either social group violates the taboos which restrict the interaction between Blacks and whites.

Jan and Mary violate these taboos from the moment they encounter Bigger. Because she is not like anyone Bigger has known before, because he knows he serves at the pleasure of her father, because he is totally ignorant of the nature of the relationship between Mary and her father, he follows her requests, taking her to meet Jan and driving them to the park instead of taking her to school. Stimulated by the alcohol they drank and hysterically confused by an evening of Jan's and Mary's attempts at intimacy and by their alien world, Bigger carries Mary to her room and responds instinctively to the appearance of blind Mrs. Dalton when he covers Mary's face with a pillow so that he can escape detection. His thoughts when he discovers that Mary is dead attest to the total authority of Mary's world and the perfunctory legal ritual of the trial that ensues: "The reality of the room fell from him; the vast city of white people that sprawled outside took its place. She was dead and he had killed her. He was a murderer, a Negro murderer, a black murderer. He had killed a white woman" (75). His premonition materializes in the breaking of the most serious of Jim Crow laws. Like Job's questioning of Jehovah, Bigger's murder of Mary challenges the most sacred code of his society. Since none of his past experiences had prepared him for Mary, fear engulfs him. "Fear," the title of Book 1, becomes a function of setting, symbolizing the effects of the environment on Bigger's psyche and emphasizing that aspect of his character which makes him succumb to the irrationality and blindness of frenzy. His fear surpasses the proportion of intimidation one person transmits to another. In magnitude, it is comparable to the terror that characterizes our response to supernatural forces we cannot explain or control.

Structurally, while the murder scene of Book 1 acts as the climax of the novel, the following two books, "Flight" and "Fate," are elements of the denouement, which charts the effects of the murder on Bigger's psyche. "Flight," the title of Book 2, illustrates how Bigger's flight from the responsibility of his crime ironically corresponds to his journey into self-awareness and self-esteem. Just as Oedipus ironically precipitates the prediction of the oracle by leaving Corinth in an attempt to escape his fate, Bigger, too, undertakes a physical journey which brings him results antithetical to his expectations. His murdering Mary diminishes his extreme fear of the white world and enables him to see himself and his family as they appear to whites. In Book 2 he begins to view his family, his friends, and the Black community with a discerning eye and a perceptivity completely alien to the Bigger of Book 1. Although the physical elements of setting in this section continue to reflect the power that whites have over Blacks, Wright shifts his emphasis. As Bigger skillfully deceives the Daltons and evades detection by the police, Wright, already having placed him against the background of his environment, focuses on the change that begins to unfold in Bigger's psyche. Bigger begins to see that the white world is trapped inside its stereotypical preconceptions of Black people and that this entrapment could be used as a weapon against that world. The pride that motivates Bigger in Book 1 incites him to use against white society the same weapon it thinks renders it secure. Thus Bigger hides his rebellion behind a shield of servility and pusillanimity. His capture at the end of Book 2, however, and his confinement and trial in Book 3 bring about another change as he is hurled into a vortex of emotional experiences that force him to complete the training that Book 2 began—to turn inward, relinquish his hostility, and accept himself for what he is. Thus the elements of setting and structure complement each other with their representation of the cause-and-effect relationship between the environment and Bigger's changing response to that environment. Book 3, suggestively titled, presents the results of the actions in Books 1 and 2, fulfilling the prophecy of environmental forces and dramatizing the change of fortune brought about by the reversal and recognition scenes characteristic of tragedy.

Since the purpose of Chapter 3 of this study is to show how Bigger Thomas's characterization and actions satisfy the criteria for tragedy, in this chapter I make only the necessary general references to those aspects of character and action that outline the plot of *Native Son*. This awkward method of separating the elements of the narrative in critical analyses can too easily falsify or ignore the artistic synthesis of fiction. Through its presentation of a world in motion, this synthesis reflects the simultaneity of the elements that make up human experience. Aristotle's explanation of the interdependent relationship of plot, action, and character elucidates the crux of the methodology which underlies tragedy and provides a basis for an analysis of Wright's controversial Book 3:

> But the most important of these is the arrangement of the incidents of the plot; for tragedy is not the portrayal of men [as such], but of action, of life. . . . Men are the certain kinds of individuals they are as a result of their character; but they become happy or miserable as a result of their actions. Consequently, dramatists do not employ action in order to achieve character portrayal, but they include character because of its relation to action. Therefore, the incidents and plot constitute the end of tragedy, and the end is the greatest thing of all. Moreover, without action there would be no tragedy, but there could be tragedy without character. (13–14)

Hence, according to Aristotle, action is the most essential element of tragedy, and character becomes important only as it reveals action. Bigger's wandering in Book 1 and the physical journey he undertakes in Book 2 as he flees from the police are replaced by the spiritual journey of Book 3. With his consciousness as the unifying principle, the incidents of the plot in Books 1 and 2 show how societal forces attempt to entrap Bigger. In Book 1 he roams in and out of his home, stands on the street, plays pool, goes to a movie, and fights with his gang before going to the Dalton home—all actions that reflect the useless routine of his life. In Book 2 the map in the newspaper which charts the approach of the vigilantes and shows that Bigger has been moving in a circle symbolizes the entrapment which typifies his life.

The action in Book 3 takes place primarily within the confines of Bigger's mind. The incidents of the plot from Book 1 through Book 3 are so arranged that the actions Bigger takes naturally thrust him deeper into his enemy's world in Book 3. His pride or indignation motivates him to refuse submission first to economic and social oppression and later to psychological oppression, manifesting the interrelationship between action and character described

by Aristotle. Bigger's psychological awakening—his awareness of
how racism has shaped his consciousness and thus his view of
himself and others—conforms to the element of the recognition,
a part of the complex plot of tragedy. He passes from "a state of ignorance into a state of knowledge," which brings a spiritual resolution characteristic of the tragic hero. Bigger's recognition—or
change of fortune—is solely a spiritual one, stemming from his act
of murdering Mary. This act catapults him into the trial, which
represents the element of reversal essential to tragedy. In his explanation of a complex action, Aristotle says that the incidents of the
plot should be so arranged that each subsequent incident occurs
according to probability. Reversal is the component of the plot
which veers the action—suggested by probability—in the opposite
direction of what is expected (21). Consequently, irony emerges as
the crux of the tragic action. Max, Bigger's Communist lawyer, is
as essential an element of the irony which comprises the reversal
in *Native Son* as the trial is.

The interaction between Max and Bigger is the final structural
component reflective of the tragic form. Bigger's recognition—his
psychological awakening—results from the trial and, more importantly, from the questions Max asks him in preparation for the
trial. Knowing that the public demands Bigger's death, Max understands that the best he can do for Bigger is to convince the judge to
forgo a death sentence for life in prison. On one level, Max is completely unsuccessful—the judge pronounces that Bigger must pay
for his crime with his life. However, satisfying Aristotle's description of the reversal, Bigger finds life in death. The trial that demands his physical death brings with it his spiritual awakening.
From the moment Max begins to prepare for Bigger's defense by
asking him questions about his past and his feelings, Max becomes
the essential agent of Bigger's awakening. Max and the effect of his
speech on Bigger's consciousness function as the structural synthesis which unites Books 1, 2, and 3, satisfying Aristotle's criterion for unity of plot in tragedy:

> . . . just as in other mimetic arts a unified imitation is an
> imitation of a single thing, in the same way the plot in trag-
> edy, since it is an imitation of action, must deal with that ac-
> tion and with the whole of it; and the different parts of the
> action must be so related to each other that if any part is
> changed or taken away the whole will be altered and dis-
> turbed. (18)

Reflecting the relationship of the part to the whole, Max's speech
addresses the environmental forces of Book 1 and Bigger's overt
challenge of these forces in Book 2.

A look at the thoughts which reveal how Max begins to break
through Bigger's iron reserve illuminates Max's role in the change
which occurs in Bigger and paves the way for our understanding of
how Bigger and Max change roles at the end of the novel. (Max's
characterization and the content of his speech will be the focus of
Chapter 5 of this study. At this point, I concentrate only on those
issues pertinent to an analysis of the general structure of the novel.)
After a long series of questions, Max leaves Bigger in an emotional
upheaval unlike anything he has ever experienced:

> Why had Max asked him all those questions? He knew that
> Max was seeking facts to tell the judge; but in Max's asking of
> those questions he had felt a recognition of his life, of his
> feelings, of his person that he had never encountered before.
> What was this? . . . He had no right to be proud; yet he had
> spoken to Max as a man who *had* something. . . .
> He wondered if it were possible that after all everybody in
> the world felt alike? Did those who hated him have in them
> the same thing Max had seen in him, the thing that had made
> Max ask him those questions? . . . For the first time in his life
> he had gained a pinnacle of feeling upon which he could stand
> and see vague relations that he had never dreamed of. . . .
> (305–6)

This long but important passage not only pinpoints Max as the
source of the power which forces Bigger to search for answers to

the meaning of his life, but also shows how Wright's characterization of Bigger transcends the narrow strictures of naturalism.

Attempting to capture the meaning of Bigger's life, Max fulfills what T. R. Henn describes as one function of the Greek chorus: "There are several methods of emphasizing the linkage between past and present. The Greek Chorus has among many functions that of conveying the sense of past momentum, and an artificial helplessness dissociated from the spectators. They are in one sense the guardians of the past, mediating, interpreting it, moralizing upon it, but never developing it into an authoritative pattern that may affect the present" (39). Analogously, Max and his speech mediate, interpret, and moralize Bigger's murder of Mary. Like the Greek chorus, Max does not affect the present—the judge's decision. Bigger, on the other hand, is stirred significantly by the mere act of Max's speech and experiences tremendous change as a result of his constant pondering of Max's earlier questions and the onslaught of emotions provoked by the trial. When Max visits Bigger immediately following the address, the narrator explains: "Bigger was not at that moment really bothered about whether Max's speech had saved his life or not. He was hugging the proud thought that Max had made the speech all for him, to save his life. It was not the meaning of the speech that gave him pride, but the mere act of it" (339).

After Buckley's address to the judge and the court's sentencing Bigger to the electric chair, Max sends Bigger a telegram explaining that the appeal to the governor had failed. When Bigger and Max meet in the final scene, the recognition and reversal are complete. Fired with the need to test his new understanding of himself in order to affirm his reality, Bigger attempts to communicate with the one person he feels will understand the many thoughts pervading his mind. The inarticulate, sullen, imprudent Bigger of Book 1 emerges in this final scene as an expressive, sensitive, and prudent young man who comprehends the role he has played in his fate through his having internalized the negative aspects of the environmental forces responsible for his present predicament. Feeling at peace with himself, he transcends the hostility fostered by these forces. His new vision, however, proves to be a hard one, in fact too hard for Max to accept. The more Bigger tries to make Max understand the reality of his life, the more Max retreats behind a wall of aloofness and resignation. The narrator's use of the word *white* in describing Max's extreme reserve in confronting Bigger evokes the previous references to the power of the white world and the ritualistic social forms that had earlier intimidated Bigger: "Max looked at him sharply and rose from his cot. He stood in front of Bigger for a moment and Bigger was on the verge of believing that Max knew, understood; but Max's next words showed him that the white man was still trying to comfort him in the face of death" (354).

No longer afraid of death, Bigger becomes the emotional aggressor, exchanging places with his counselor, Max. Bigger perceives that Max is unable to accept his proclamation: "I didn't want to kill! . . . But what I killed for, I *am*! It must've been pretty deep in me to make me kill! I must have felt it awful hard to murder . . ." (358). Max—who earlier himself in his address called Bigger's murder of Mary an "act of *creation*"—reveals, through his repulsion of Bigger's starkly realistic acceptance of that same action, his superficial, perfunctory performance of his duty in defending Bigger. He does not take seriously the initial talk he had with Bigger and thus forgets that he derived the idea for terming the murder an "act of *creation*" from the information he collected from Bigger.

Bigger, the hero, assumes a caring role. He understands that Max's political performance does not reach the level of emotional approval which would enable Max to accept the horrors that underlie Bigger's particular reality. Sewall's explanation of the ironic reversal of roles between Job and the Counselors analogously enriches our understanding of this final scene in *Native Son*:

> Nothing is more revealing of Job's (and the tragic hero's) stature than the contrast which the Poet develops between Job and the Counselors. Job outstrips them in every way. By chap-

ter 28 Job has achieved an ironic reversal of roles: the Counselors who came to teach him are being taught by him—and on the subject of Wisdom. He fails to convince them of the injustice of his suffering or even of the possibility of a flaw in their pat theology. But in failing to change their minds he demonstrates the littleness of minds that cannot be changed. He grows in stature as they shrink. He knows that he has achieved a vision, through suffering, beyond anything they can know. (20)

Chapter 3 will focus on Bigger's suffering and trace the development of his vision, concentrating on the pride that spurs his defiance, induces his suffering, and is thus ultimately responsible for the wisdom he achieves before his death. The Bigger who once ached because he was too afraid to move his legs while sitting between two whites and whose most frequent response to whites was either "Nawsuh" or "Yessuh," says to Max, "Tell . . . Tell Mister . . . Tell Jan hello. . . ." In order to appreciate the full significance of Bigger's change, the reader must hold in mind that the epithet *mister*, which a Black man must use in addressing a male representative of the white world, is as prominent a commandment in a Jim Crow society as the taboo restricting interaction between Black men and white women.

The three-sentence final paragraph of the novel affirms the interrelationship Wright has skillfully sustained between setting and structure. After Bigger and Max say good-bye, the narrator says about Bigger: "He still held on to the bars. Then he smiled a faint, wry, bitter smile. He heard the ring of steel against steel as a far door clanged shut" (359). The ringing sound of steel against steel that reverberates in Bigger's and the reader's ears echoes Bigger's mother's admonishment as to his fate as well as his own premonitions. The steel door appropriately represents the power of the white world that has sought to subdue Bigger. Having in one sense come full circle, Bigger now awaits his impending death, which results from the overwhelming fear that characterizes him in Book 1 and from his challenge of the white world at the end of Book 1 and throughout Book 2. Consequently, with the development of Bigger's consciousness at the center of the novel, the elements of setting become integral components of structure. His "faint, wry, bitter smile" illuminates the depth of his suffering and the irony that pervades the entire novel. For everyone assumes that Bigger's real crime is rape, not murder. We are left with conflicting feelings as we, like Bigger, understand that his spiritual awakening comes just at the point when he is condemned to die.

3. Characterization and Point of View: The Tragic Hero

igger's predestined outcome, embodied in the elements of setting and the series of events that leads to his incarceration, illuminate him as the tragic hero. For he is alienated from both the Black and white communities because of his volatile, stubborn, determined, prideful personality. This portrayal of Bigger challenges the stereotypical images of most Black characters prior to 1940 and the traditional assumption that victimized characters and tragic heroes are mutually exclusive.

At the outset of his "Blueprint for Negro Writing," Wright addresses what he sees as the need of Black writers to depict Black characters that move beyond the limits of stereotypes and racial expectations:

> Generally speaking, Negro writing in the past has been confined to humble novels, poems, and plays, prim and decorous ambassadors who went a-begging to white America. They entered the Court of American Public Opinion dressed in the knee-pants of servility, curtsying to show that the Negro was not inferior, that he was human, and that he had a life comparable to that of other people. For the most part these artistic ambassadors were received as though they were French poodles who do clever tricks. (37)

Ironically, this statement subtly undercuts the mistaken notion that Wright's depiction of Bigger Thomas is merely a plea for Black humanity and speaks to the need of Black literature to represent truthfully the complicated consciousness of Black Americans. With Bigger Thomas's psyche at its center, *Native Son* describes a young man who, when unaware of his emotional victimization, succumbs to the hysteria of racial oppression and who, after becoming conscious of his fears and emotional blindness, understands the role he has played in his suffering. Thus in his characterization of Bigger, Wright probes deep into human consciousness, revealing the intricacies of Bigger's personality that make him at once good and evil, fearful and defiant, awful and awesome.

This rendering of Bigger through these juxtapositions of opposites manifests itself in Wright's denunciation of the portrayals of Blacks as simple one-dimensional figures. For Wright clearly understood that to depict Black life in the midst of a vortex of social, political, and economic impediments does not demand that the depictions of Black people be stereotypical or predominately reflections of victimization. An example of the dehumanizing effects of racial oppression and of the strength and ambiguity which the human spirit embodies, Bigger emerges as a rebellious, prideful, temperamental, challenging young hero whose suffering and emotional growth result from his refusal to acquiesce to the racial injustices of a Jim Crow society. The initial scenes of the novel make evident what becomes a most essential element of Bigger's personality: the interrelationship between his rebellious spirit and his strong sense of pride. Bigger's pride, which is apparent when we first meet him, undergirds the sullen indifference that typifies his interaction with his family and gang in Book 1, motivates his rebelliousness in Book 2, and awakens him at the beginning of Book 3.

As the title of Book 1 suggests, fear proves to be as strong an element of Bigger's personality as his pride. When confronted with the white world or with merely a suggestion of confrontation, Bigger most often becomes completely enwrapped by fear. This fear, which surfaces in Bigger's loss of control, is his *hamartia*, his mistake in judgment or the force responsible for his error in judgment. Throughout the novel, Bigger vacillates between indifference bolstered by his strong sense of pride and hysteria incited by his equally intense fear of the white world. Both immobility and fear engulf him as he accidentally murders Mary Dalton. Yet, despite this fear and the numerous opportunities he has to flee for his life before the discovery of Mary's bones, he defiantly remains among the Daltons, controlling and manipulating them through his awareness of the discrepancy between his reality and their illusions concerning that reality. The discovery that he is Mary's murderer results only from his loss of control—his inability to sustain a balance between fear and his new insight into the vulnerability of the white world. It is characteristic of tragedy that the same personality trait which accentuates the hero's humanness ironically precipitates his downfall—in this case Bigger's mistakes in judgment that lead to his murders, capture, and impending death.

Those passages in which Bigger's fear overwhelms his judgment and precipitates immobility, hysteria, or violence highlight the function of a third-person limited narrator who makes evident Bigger's thoughts, motives, and the subtle shifts in his consciousness. Since Wright's purpose is to present a work "so hard and deep that [his readers] would have to face it without the consolation of tears," his most difficult task is that of achieving an artistic balance between the aesthetic distance necessary to avoid excessive pity and the empathy necessary to ensure the reader's admiration of Bigger's determination and spiritual awakening. The third-person point of view resolves this dilemma through its relationship with characterization. For Wright's central intelligence softens the impact of Bigger's volatile temperament and his tendency toward violence. Rather than illuminating a contradiction in Wright's intention to maintain an aesthetic distance, the third-person center of consciousness reflects instead the degree to which Wright—the tragic artist—commits himself to sustaining the tension throughout the thrust and parry of the ideas that embody Bigger's fate (Sewall 13).

Susanne Langer's "The Tragic Rhythm" succinctly summarizes the movement of tragic drama, providing insight into the movement of *Native Son* as well as into the essence of Wright's depiction of Bigger:

> Tragic drama is so designed that the protagonist grows mentally, emotionally, or morally, by the demand of the action,

which he himself initiated, to the complete exhaustion of his powers, the limit of his possible development. He spends himself in the course of one dramatic action. This is, of course, a tremendous foreshortening of life; instead of undergoing the physical and psychical, many-sided, long process of an actual biography, the tragic hero lives and matures in some particular respect; his entire being is concentrated in one aim, one passion, one conflict and ultimate defeat. (90)

Wright, like the many tragedians before him, begins *Native Son* at a point in which the elements of his hero's past have already conspired to bring about Bigger's "ultimate defeat." The seeds of Bigger's destiny and his challenge of his fate are rooted in his obstinacy in taking the job at the Daltons'. Consequently, quite early in Book 1, the job with the Daltons becomes the essential element of the dramatic action through which Bigger's characterization unfolds.

Bigger's resistance in accepting a job given to him by the relief office separates him emotionally from his family and friends as much as it does from the white world that provides the job. His aggressive slaughter of the huge rat, his dangling the rat in his sister's face, his habit of lying to his mother, and his routine fights with members of his gang exemplify his volatile temperament and rebelliousness long before he meets Mary Dalton. Distinctly different from the rest of his family and friends, Bigger is unable to acquiesce to the socioeconomic rules that govern the conditions in his home and in the rest of his community. His resentment of his family's stifled lives provokes his challenge of the Jim Crow codes that dominate their existence. His rebellious actions and pride consistently place him in opposition to the white world in a manner similar to that of the relationship between the Greeks and their gods: "To the Greeks, every action was a risk because it might invite the displeasure of a god; but, such was the tragic aspect of existence, man had to act. Great actions, the kind about which tragedies were written, involved great risks; and, since they inevitably involved a degree of *hubris*, they were ambiguous" (Sewall

35–36). Wright's descriptions of Bigger in the early scenes depict a young man whose proximity to whites is not only a risk to himself but also to those whites with whom he interacts. The explosive combination of Bigger's lack of exposure to whites, his rebelliousness, and his fear exacerbates the risks involved when he becomes employed in the Dalton home.

Bigger's actions reflect the ambiguity of his personality. The same pride that forces him to challenge the established order of things also bolsters his sullenness and the seeming indifference that hides his feelings. The narrator's descriptions of Bigger's thoughts after he upsets his entire family reveal the ambiguity in Bigger's character by highlighting the discrepancy between his awareness of the tenuous condition of his family and his response to this condition:

> He shut their voices out of his mind. He hated his family because he knew that they were suffering and that he was powerless to help them. He knew that the moment he allowed himself to feel to its fulness how they lived, the shame and misery of their lives, he would be swept out of himself with fear and despair. So he held toward them an attitude of iron reserve. . . . he denied himself and acted tough. (9)

Suggesting the naturalness of Bigger's personality, Wright compares the aura of a flower that blooms mysteriously to the response Bigger's family and friends have toward his moods and sullen temperament. For his family and friends never know exactly how Bigger will respond to a given situation. His pride motivates him to action and sets him apart from the rest of the Blacks in the novel. He hates and fears himself as he observes his behavior from a distance, but is unable to control himself because the hate and fear are so strong.

Bigger's accidental murder of Mary is an inevitable outcome of the socioeconomic elements of a Jim Crow society. However, his strong sense of pride and courageous spirit distinguish him significantly—tragically—from the typical naturalistic character.

Sewall's description of Oedipus's *hubris* and the unfolding of Oedipus's fate aptly applies to Bigger: "A man without *hubris* would have humbly acquiesced in his fate and let it unfold as it would. There would have been no significant action" (37). Instead of humbly acquiescing, Bigger responds to Mary's death by taking control of his life and thrusting himself deeper into the tragic experience.

Emboldened by his own daring exploits in disposing of Mary's body and by his skillful manipulation of the Daltons and the police, Bigger challenges the stereotypical image of his blackness. Though Mary's murder, his framing Jan, his writing the kidnap note, and his implicating the Communist party all attest to his rebelliousness, the courage he displays during the final scene of Book 1, his capture, demonstrates his intensity, his "will to do or die, the uncompromising spirit which makes him pay any price, even life itself, for his object" (Myers 135).

Wet and soiled from urinating in his clothes upon hitting the snow when he jumped out of the window of his room, hungry, almost frozen, frightened, and hysterically desperate for many hours, Bigger defiantly struggles to escape the hostile vigilantes. His reaction to the long awaited "There he is!" that signals his being spotted on the roof of a ramshackle building reflects a determination—characteristic of the tragic hero—to fight with every inch of his life: "The three words made him stop; he had been listening for them all night and when they came he seemed to feel the sky crashing soundlessly about him. What was the use of running? Would it not be better to stop, stand up, and lift his hands high above his head in surrender? Hell, naw! He continued to crawl" (224).

It is no accident that the first person from Bigger's community to visit him in jail is Reverend Hammond. Just as most Blacks in Bigger's community see themselves through the distorted images presented in the newspapers, they have also internalized the image of themselves as downtrodden, fated sufferers following the life of Christ. Thus Reverend Hammond's mission is to render Bigger submissive. Bigger, however, unlike his mother and the rest of his environment, rejects religion and its concomitant passivity and guilt. He is a man of action and necessity. For "he had killed within himself the preacher's haunting picture of life even before he had killed Mary; that had been his first murder" (242). Bigger has long intuitively recognized that the white world uses religion as a kind of sedative that minimizes rebelliousness in Blacks. Bigger's adverse reaction to religion corresponds to what D. D. Raphael sees as the tragic hero's necessary defiance of religion: "Because Tragedy snatches a spiritual victory out of a natural defeat, it is nearer to the religious attitude than is Epic. In another way, however, Tragedy tends to be inimical to religion. It elevates man in his struggle with necessity, while the religious attitude is one of abasement before that which is greater than man, before the awe-inspiring sublime" (196).

In addition to Bigger's rejection of religion, his murder of Bessie is another element of necessity which characterizes him as a tragic hero. His thoughts when he equates Bessie's alcohol with his mother's religion pinpoint his isolation from the rest of the community by emphasizing his will for the ideal—in this case social and economic retribution:

> He hated his mother for that way of hers which was like Bessie's. What his mother had was Bessie's whiskey, and Bessie's whiskey was his mother's religion. He did not want to sit on a bench and sing, or lie in a corner and sleep. It was when he read the newspapers or magazines, went to the movies, or walked along the streets with crowds, that he felt what he wanted: to merge himself with others and be a part of this world, to lose himself in it so he could find himself, to be allowed a chance to live like others, even though he was black. (204)

Ironically, Bigger's rebellious will to act in response to the socioeconomic restraints that preclude his being an integral part of American society further separates him from his family, friends, and the mainstream of American society.

Bessie's death clinches his rejection of the social norm of his environment. Her relationship to him and the feeling this relationship evokes in the reader call to mind Northrop Frye's description of the female suppliant necessary to enhance the tragic mood. After discussing the *bomolochos*, or comic character that increases the comic mood, Frye continues:

> The corresponding contrasting type in tragedy is the suppliant, the character, often female, who presents a picture of unmitigated helplessness and destitution. Such a figure is pathetic, and pathos, though it seems a gentler and more relaxed mood than tragedy, is even more terrifying. Its basis is the exclusion of an individual from a group, hence it attacks the deepest fear in ourselves that we possess. . . . In the figure of the suppliant pity and terror are brought to the highest possible pitch of intensity, and the awful consequences of rejecting the suppliant for all concerned is a central theme of Greek tragedy. Suppliant figures are often women threatened with death or rape. . . . (217)

Consequently, Bigger's rape and apparent superfluous murder of Bessie emerge as essential elements of Wright's tragic theme. Wright characterizes Bigger as the single individual who, through his preordained murder of Mary Dalton, is catapulted into taking control of his own life. The scene in which Bigger's mother, sister, brother, Jack, G. H., Gus, Buckley, Jan, Max, and the Daltons crowd around Bigger in a single room suggests that these characters are a kind of chorus "against which the hero's hybris may be measured" (Frye 109).

Bigger's *hubris* incites the defiance which underlies his strategy to remain in the Dalton home and to orchestrate the movement of his own destiny. He replaces his knife and gun, the previous symbols of his rebellion, with a new type of weapon—his awareness of the discrepancy between his reality and the white world's perception of him. This new insight stimulates Bigger's imagination and gives him self-confidence for the first time in his life. He assumes the role of the subversive strategist who comes to know his enemy far better than his enemy understands him. When questioned about

Mary's absence by Mrs. Dalton, he quickly intuits the sociological and racist codes that prohibit Mrs. Dalton from searching below the surface of things: ". . . he knew that a certain element of shame would keep Mrs. Dalton from asking him too much and letting him know that she was worried. He was a boy and she was an old woman. He was the hired and she was the hirer. . . . After all, he was black and she was white. He was poor and she was rich" (108–9). And later when Bigger meets Britten, Mr. Dalton's private detective, Bigger effaces his intelligence, assuming a docile attitude that fulfills Britten's expectations. Bigger understands Britten on sight and slowly feeds him the information he wants him to have.

Chance affords Bigger a number of opportunities to attempt an escape long before his capture. Like the typical tragic hero, however, he plunges deeper into the tragic experience, choosing not only to fight, but also to shape his destiny. As he carries Mary's trunk to the car in his perfunctory move of taking it to the train station, he contemplates leaving with the money he had taken from Mary's purse. But self-confidence and excitement motivate his decision to test his will to its extreme. And even after Britten's hostile, intense interrogation, Bigger gathers his defiant forces, determined to outwit his adversaries:

> Bigger went to the window and looked out at the white curtain of falling snow. He thought of the kidnap note. Should he try to get money from them now? Hell, yes! He would show that Britten bastard! . . . He'd give that Britten something to worry about, all right. Just wait.
>
> Because he could go now, run off if he wanted to and leave it all behind, he felt a certain sense of power, a power born of a latent capacity to live. (140)

The series of events that unfolds once Bigger reaches the Dalton home gives him the opportunity to take the risk which pushes to the surface his hidden potential to pursue life to its fullest, to push himself in order to discover his greatest possibilities. By showing Bigger's rebellious nature, which has always isolated him from the

Black community and branded him a threat to the white community, Wright depicts Bigger as the hero whose desires exceed the limitations peculiar to a Jim Crow society.

No matter how well planned, Bigger's crafty strategy is destined for failure. The success of his choice of action depends upon his ability to control his fear, and ironically it is this fear which causes him to lose control and thus precipitates his capture. Although malevolent external forces play an essential role in setting the tragic pattern in motion (Delmar 4), Bigger's psychological makeup is responsible for the errors in judgment that produce and sustain the tragic action. In the initial scenes, Bigger's sullen treatment of his family and the violent display of emotions that instigates the fight with Gus spring from his fear. In the case of his family, Bigger assumes a sullen persona because he fears the vulnerability of love and responsibility.

Quite simply, he fights with Gus because he fears whites intensely. In describing Bigger's feelings as he waits for Gus to agree to rob their first white store-owner, the narrator explains how Bigger transfers his fear of whites to violence toward Gus:

> He hated Gus because he knew that Gus was afraid, as even he was; and he feared Gus because he felt that Gus would consent and then he would be compelled to go through with the robbery. . . . he watched Gus and waited for him to say yes. . . . Then he could not stand it any longer. The hysterical tensity of his nerves urged him to speak, to free himself. He faced Gus, his eyes red with anger and fear, his fists clenched and held stiffly to his sides. (22)

The contradiction between Bigger's fear of robbing a white man and the fact that he himself is the originator of the idea to rob Blum reflects the irreconcilable aspects of his personality. He vacillates between fear and hate, hate and shame, sullenness and hysteria.

Just as his loss of control with Gus alienates him completely from his gang, the hysteria which overcomes him when Mrs. Dalton enters Mary's room brings about Mary's death. Bigger's fear of whites, and their lack of perception of how environmental forces have shaped their psyches quite differently from his, function conjointly to presage Bigger's murder of Mary. The scenes that portray Bigger's contempt for Mary as she naively questions him about unions and communism, and his extreme discomfort with Jan and Mary in Ernie's Kitchen Shack, all stimulate in Bigger a desire to "leap" to action to destroy the emotions that overwhelm him. Wright's frequent use of the word *leap* in describing Bigger when he feels most entrapped and the imagery that compares Bigger's feelings to the processes of nature suggest that Bigger reacts instinctively when confronted with a representative of the world that seeks to dominate him.

Bigger understands that being in Mary Dalton's room automatically means that he has broken the most important law of the cosmological order characteristic of a Jim Crow society. Consequently, when blind Mrs. Dalton enters Mary's room, Bigger completely loses control as his fear powerfully overwhelms him. When Mrs. Dalton approaches the bed, he becomes caught up in a spell of hysteria, intuitively acting to save his life. Throughout this scene that moves very quickly, Wright charts Bigger's reactions so vividly that a careful reading of the scene precludes any idea that Bigger acts with evil intent. As Mary tries to rise from the bed in response to her mother's voice,

> *Frenzy* dominated him. He held his hand over her mouth and his head was cocked at an angle that enabled him to see Mary and Mrs. Dalton by merely shifting his eyes. Mary mumbled and tried to rise again. *Frantically* he caught a corner of the pillow and brought it to her lips. He had to stop her from mumbling, or he would be caught. Mrs. Dalton was moving slowly toward him and he grew tight and full, as though about to explode. Mary's fingernails tore at his hands and he caught the pillow and covered her entire face with it firmly. . . .
>
> His eyes were filled with the white blur moving toward him in the shadows of the room. Again Mary's body heaved and he held the pillow in a grip that took all of his strength. . . .

He clenched his teeth and held his breath, intimidated to the core by the awesome white blur floating toward him. His muscles flexed taut as steel and he pressed the pillow, feeling the bed give slowly, evenly, but silently. (73–74, emphasis mine)

One of the most important scenes in the novel, this necessarily long passage demonstrates the intensity of Bigger's fear and shows the extent to which fear holds him in a trance, causing him literally to lose sight of everything around him, except the "white blur."

Ironically, then, Bigger's act of carrying Mary to her room to save himself from blame and harm backfires cataclysmically. Of more importance, and equally ironic, is the fact that the failure of his attempts to defy his destiny is in part rooted in his own psyche. As long as he maintains his self-control, he is able to sustain the emotional stability and strength he needs to meet any sudden, unexpected change. Any arousal of fear renders him vulnerable and ineffectual. The furnace, which continually excites his fear to an intensity comparable to that responsible for his murder of Mary, is the curse or mistake that instigates Bigger's capture. Like his fear of whites, fear of the furnace rhythmically presages danger and entrapment. When he carries Mary's body to the basement, he intends to dispose of her by using the trunk until he spontaneously decides to burn her in the furnace. His burning Mary compounds the levels of irony that lead to his incarceration. For both his fear of the furnace and the lingering images of Mary's body haunt him and finally cause him to become so immobilized that he pinpoints himself as her murderer.

His crucial mistake in judgment is his delay in cleaning the furnace. Because of his intense fear of attracting attention to the furnace, he permits the coal to pile up, knowing that the ashes could eventually block the air ducts:

He stood a moment looking through the cracks into the humming fire, blinding red now. But how long would it keep that

> way, if he did not shake the ashes down? He remembered the
> last time he had tried and how hysterical he had felt. . . . He
> imagined that if he shook it he would see pieces of bone fall-
> ing into the bin and he knew that he would not be able to en-
> dure it. He jerked upright and, lashed by fiery whips of fear
> and guilt, backed hurriedly to the door. . . . he could not bring
> himself to shake those ashes. (145–46)

Bigger continues to stall, hoping that the reporters and Britten will
leave the house. Instead of leaving, the reporters, excited by the
coverage of Mary's absence in their daily papers, decide to question
Bigger again and to take pictures of him and the Daltons. When it
gets cool in the house, the moment finally arrives when Peggy, as
she brings coffee to the reporters, asks Bigger to clean the ashes.

Her request confounds Bigger as much as the shepherd's story of
Oedipus's past befuddles Oedipus. Bigger's first thoughts reveal his
emotions: "Clean the fire out! Good God! Not now, not with the
men standing round" (182). The movements that follow progress as
quickly and as intensely as those of the rat scene. Bigger gradually
loses control. Against all his will, he knows he has to respond to
Peggy's order because the other whites have heard her. He opens
the door to the storage bin and decides to add more coal, hoping
that the fire will burn until the basement is free of the reporters.
On the contrary, the smoke burgeons rapidly, choking him, filling
the room, and stifling the reporters. When a reporter frantically
takes the shovel, Bigger knows that he no longer has control of
the situation: "He wanted to go to him and ask for the shovel; he
wanted to say that he could take care of it now. But he did not
move. He felt that he had let things slip through his hands to such
an extent that he could not get at them again" (184). When the reporter with the shovel stares incredulously into the ashes, Bigger's
worst fear materializes. Wright compares Bigger's feelings to the
malfunctioning of the furnace, suggesting the symbolic relationship between Bigger's fear and the furnace: "Bigger edged forward,
his lungs not taking in or letting out air; he himself was a huge
furnace now through which no air could go; and the fear that

surged into his stomach, filling him, choking him, was like the fumes of smoke that had belched from the ash bin" (185). Overwhelmed by the fear responsible for his error in judgment, Bigger again attempts to defy his destiny. While the reporters are entranced by what they find in the ashes, Bigger escapes.

Although we do not sanction his murder of Mary, we empathize with him because of the intense fear that motivates his actions. Thus, characteristic of tragedy, Bigger's *hamartia*—his loss of control caused by fear—plays the paradoxical role of making him at once vulnerably human and threateningly awesome. Despite our knowing that Bigger's fate and our moral code demand that he be captured, we become involved in his struggle to evade the vigilantes. For Wright's adroit use of a third-person limited narrator controls the degree to which we identify with Bigger's tragedy. Katherine Fishburn summarizes the function of the narrator in *Native Son*: ". . . *Native Son* is told entirely from the viewpoint of Bigger Thomas, the narrator; we never know what is in the minds of other characters. In limiting himself to Bigger's perspective, Wright is asking the reader to identify with his hero and to try to understand his motives and actions" (12). The role of the narrator is to soften the reader's harsh judgment of Bigger by establishing an affinity between the reader's consciousness and Bigger's, and thus ensuring that we feel Bigger's fate as our own. The tragic artist traditionally creates a hero whose courage and defiance incite our admiration and censure. We censure the hero when his actions offend our sensibilities and separate us from him, and we admire him— from a sublime distance—as he fights in the face of all adversity.

Although the narrator identifies completely with Bigger, as Fishburn explains, he is not to be confused with Bigger. Because Bigger is inarticulate and incommunicative throughout most of the novel, the narrator reveals the seething world of Bigger's psyche, illuminating motives and thoughts Bigger fails to perceive. Vacillating between extreme sullenness and an explosive temper, Bigger lacks the introspection that brings self-knowledge. The narrator "at the most crucial points of action and self-recognition, becomes a sort of translator, or refiner, of the stifled, muddled intensity of Bigger's inner life" (Larsen 106). With the exception of Bigger's murder of Mary, the essential action in *Native Son* takes place in Bigger's mind. This internal counteraction functions—by means of the narrator—as an element of the tragic dialectic through which the effects of Bigger's suffering unfold.

An informed, keen, and sensitive narrator provides the comprehensive look at Bigger's thoughts, revealing the reasons for the sullen moods, iron reserve, volatile temperament, and fear which characterize Bigger in Book 1. After Bigger kills Mary, the narrator, throughout Book 2, intermittently directs attention to the emotional battle that takes place in Bigger's mind. At the same time that he struggles defiantly to forge his own destiny by outwitting the Daltons and the police, Bigger fights a battle to overcome the guilt and stress that persistently threaten him. While his fear of the furnace is the final cause of his loss of control, the haunting image of Mary's bloody head also works to subdue him. Complementing the narrator's explanation of Bigger's motives, the references to the lingering images of Mary's body help to counterbalance the portrayal of Bigger's violent nature and thus mitigate against the reader's harsh judgment of him.

Working against the strength that manifests itself when Bigger faces the Daltons and Britten, the images of Mary's head become opposing internal forces that reflect the divisive personality characteristic of the tragic hero. These recurring images highlight the seething emotional turbulence hidden by Bigger's mask of composure. When he approaches the furnace and imagines that he sees Mary's head, he risks losing his mask:

> The inside of the furnace breathed and quivered in the grip of fiery coals. But there was no sign of the body, even though the body's image hovered before his eyes, between his eyes and the bed of coals burning hotly. . . .
> At the moment he stooped to grasp the protruding handle of the lower bin to shake it to and fro, a vivid image of Mary's face as he had seen it upon the bed in the blue light of the

room gleamed at him from the smoldering embers and he rose abruptly, giddy and hysterical with guilt and fear. His hands twitched. . . . (100–101)

This picture of Bigger's vulnerability serves the same functions as the narrator's description of the fear and mixed emotions Bigger experiences in his home and with his gang. Outwardly tough and intractable in his attitude toward his family and friends, and manipulative and shrewd in his treatment of the Daltons and the police, Bigger is always inwardly quite fearful and neurotic.

The relationship between the image of Mary's head and Bigger's increasing anxiety reaches its peak in a bizarre dream which discloses the depth of Bigger's apprehensions. After Britten initially interrogates him, Bigger, physically and emotionally exhausted, slips into a deep sleep in which he dreams he hears a ringing church bell that grows louder as he stands on a street corner. He stands in a red glare like the glare from the furnace, holding a heavy, wet, and slippery package. When he unwraps the package, he discovers his own head with wet bloody hair. When white people begin to close in on him asking questions about the head, he awakes slowly, realizing that the sound is coming from the doorbell of his room. From the moment the bell begins to ring directly over Bigger's head, Wright describes how Bigger's waking fears reflect his unconsciousness. The approximately 316 unpunctuated words of Bigger's dream diminish the emotional barriers between Bigger's unconscious mind and our own.

Wright achieves a skillful balance between those elements which evoke the reader's identification with Bigger and those that detach us from him. The narrator's astute translations of Bigger's thoughts as well as the numerous descriptions of Bigger's emotional and physical fatigue counteract our response to the repugnant scenes in which Bigger chops off Mary's head with the hatchet and batters Bessie's face with a brick. Even Bigger's daring, hardened attempts to carry out his scheme of collecting money by using the kidnap note are accompanied by the narrator's intermittent descriptions of Bigger's nervousness and extreme exhaustion. When Bessie deduces why Bigger is certain that Mary will not show up to thwart his plans of collecting the kidnap money, the narrator calls attention to the change Bessie's recognition of Bigger as a murderer effects in him:

> His jaw clamped tight and he stood up. . . . He began to feel cold; he discovered that his body was covered with sweat. He heard a soft rustle and looked down at his hand; the kidnap note was shaking in his trembling fingers. But I ain't scared, he told himself. He folded the note, put it into an envelope, sealed it by licking the flap, and shoved it in his pocket. (151)

Hence despite his fear, exhaustion, and the odds against him, Bigger is a man driven by the necessity to test his power.

In fact, Bigger's will is so strong that we tend to overlook the implications inherent in the narrator's descriptions of Bigger's struggle to avoid collapsing. After Bigger slips the kidnap note under the Daltons' door and burns the gloves and pencil and paper, physical weakness, fear, and anxiety sap his strength, illuminating his loneliness and agonizing sense of guilt:

> A strange sensation enveloped him. Something tingled in his stomach and on his scalp. His knees wobbled, giving way. He stumbled to the wall and leaned against it weakly. A wave of numbness spread fanwise from his stomach over his entire body, including his head and eyes, making his mouth gap. Strength ebbed from him. He sank to his knees and pressed his fingers to the floor to keep from tumbling over. An organic sense of dread seized him. His teeth chattered and he felt sweat sliding down his armpits and back. He groaned, holding as still as possible. His vision was blurred; but gradually it cleared. Again he saw the furnace. Then he realized that he had been on the verge of collapse. (157–58)

Bigger's exhaustion and loneliness grow as he fights for his freedom. With Bessie, before her death, as his only marginal companion, he is enwrapped by an "organic sense of dread" and is unable to sleep and eat.

He runs to Bessie not only for the money from Mary's purse, but also because he yearns for companionship. Thus his initial thoughts are not of murder. But while he is in Bessie's presence, her cowering makes him see that including her in his plans has been a mistake. His realization of the necessity to kill Bessie comes to him suddenly and firmly from the depths of consciousness: "He wondered if she was sleeping; somewhere deep in him he knew that he was lying here waiting for her to go to sleep. Bessie did not figure in what was before him" (199). He fidgets with the brick, the flashlight, and the blanket, delaying the act that he himself finds totally repugnant. The narrator carefully explains that Bigger's heart beats wildly, his breath swells, and his muscles flex as he tries "to impose his will over his body." Only his thoughts of Mary's burning body, of Britten, and of the law help him overcome his revulsion at the idea of killing Bessie.

After Bessie's death, Bigger flees through and across the tops of apartment buildings, trying to evade capture. Throughout these scenes that lead to Bigger's incarceration, the narrator persistently points to Bigger's isolation and loneliness and describes the effects of his hunger and of the cold, icy water from the fire hose that finally whirls him onto his back. Still functioning as an essential means of sustaining a balance between the opposing aspects of Bigger's personality, the narrator at the beginning of Book 3 becomes obtrusive because Bigger is in a semiconscious state and because he grapples with ideas completely new to him. And near the end of the novel, the narrator virtually disappears when Bigger, stimulated by Max's questions that plunge him deep into introspection and retrospection, begins to articulate his own feelings. The articulate, pensive, tranquil Bigger who emerges from Book 3 is quite different from the sullen, temperamental, neurotic young man who reports to work at the Dalton home. Bigger's suffering yields knowledge and is responsible for the change in character Sewall holds necessary to tragedy: "One simple criterion of tragedy lies in the question, How does our first view of the protagonist . . . differ from what we see at the end? Has there been a gain, if only minimal, in humanity, self-knowledge, wisdom, insight—all that we have subsumed under the notion of perception?" (167)

The price that Bigger must pay for his new knowledge of self is suffering and death. The change that he undergoes begins, of course, when he takes the job at the Daltons' and continues as he struggles to escape the police. His incarceration in Book 3 enhances his suffering and catapults him into a vortex of new emotions that lead to his discovery of self-awareness. Pride forces him to attempt again to control his own life. Traditionally, pride is the tragic flaw that makes the hero vulnerable to the forces that attempt to subdue him and ironically precipitates his transcendence.

The inquest scene which opens Book 3 brings Bigger closer to his fate. Having failed in his attempt to bring meaning into his life, he yearns to reach inside himself to destroy that which gave him hope. His coma symbolizes his "deep physiological resolution not to react to anything" (233). Because Bigger is only semiconscious and because his confinement brings him into the realm of completely new experiences, the narrator plays a key role in interpreting Bigger's feelings. He even goes so far as to explain that Bigger cannot intellectualize his feelings of renunciation; instead, "this feeling sprang up of itself, organically, automatically; like the rotted hull of a seed forming the soil in which it should grow again" (234).

Bigger's organic desire to pull completely inward, to kill himself, is as instinctive as the indignation that forces him to consciousness when he perceives that the purpose of the inquest is to mock and demean him. The narrator describes Bigger's movement toward consciousness and rebellion as he watches those around him in the large room of the Cook County Morgue:

> There was in the air a silent mockery that challenged him. It was not their hate he felt; it was something deeper than that. He sensed that in their attitude toward him they had gone beyond hate. . . . Though he could not put it into words, he felt that not only had they resolved to put him to death, but that they were determined to make his death mean more than a mere punishment. . . . And as he felt it, rebellion rose in him. He had sunk to the lowest point this side of death, but when

> he felt his life again threatened in a way that meant that he
> was to go down the dark road a helpless spectacle of sport
> for others, he sprang back into action, alive, contending.
> (235–36)

The same rebellious attitude and pride that characterize Bigger in Books 1 and 2 spring him back to consciousness with a new determination to defy the powerful, capricious forces that challenge his self-respect.

This time his pride forces him to do battle in an emotional arena rather than a physical one. During the course of his confinement, his consciousness grows in depth and perceptivity. Although Bigger's initial response to Max does not differ significantly from his reaction to Buckley or any of the whites around him, he eventually responds to Max's questions, which are designed to extract from him the reasons for the drives and fears that made him react so intensely as to kill. When Bigger first feels the urge to talk, his inexperience at self-evaluation thwarts him:

> Bigger was staring straight before him, his eyes wide and
> shining. His talking to Max had evoked again in him that
> urge to talk, to tell, to try to make his feelings known. A wave
> of excitement flooded him. He felt that he ought to be able to
> reach out with his bare hands and carve from naked space the
> concrete, solid reasons why he had murdered. He felt them
> that strongly. If he could do that, he would relax; he would sit
> and wait until they told him to walk to the chair; and he
> would walk. (295–96)

This passage punctuates Bigger's emerging need to establish some link between himself and the rest of humanity and his desire to discover, for the first time in his life, who he is so that he might die with dignity.

His drive to communicate places him inside the world. Lying on his cot and reflecting upon the events of his life, he begins to understand that he has never been as unconnected to others as he had thought. After his family visits him in jail and relates the Black and white communities' maltreatment of them in response to Bigger's crimes, he realizes that his life indeed affects the well-being of his family. This discovery of a link with something outside himself, along with Max's subsequent questions, unleashes thoughts and feelings that had been unfamiliar to Bigger. Explaining Bigger's thoughts after a long session with Max, the narrator reveals Bigger's trepidation at the new thoughts forming within him:

> For the first time in his life he had gained a pinnacle of feeling upon which he could stand and see vague relations that he had never dreamed of. If that white looming mountain of hate were not a mountain at all, but people, people like himself, and like Jan—then he was faced with a high hope the like of which he had never thought could be, and a despair the full depths of which he knew he could not stand to feel. (306)

Bigger, however, is not able "to leave this newly seen and newly felt thing alone" (306).

The entire experience of the trial and the physical limitations that confinement places upon Bigger thrust him even deeper into self-analysis. Although he does not comprehend the words in Max's speech, the mere act of the speech and Max's seeming sincerity move Bigger to want "to talk with him and feel with as much keenness as possible what his living and dying meant" (350). During this last scene in which both Bigger and Max face each other with the knowledge that the governor has refused Bigger's appeal, Bigger's self-revelation reveals the outcome of the long emotional battle that has characterized him in Book 3.

In a long and powerful speech that demonstrates Bigger's growth and makes it clear that a subtle change has taken place in the relationship between him and the narrator, the new Bigger evinces that his suffering has yielded the knowledge of his affinity with the rest of mankind:

> "Mr. Max, I sort of saw myself after that night. And I sort of saw other people, too." Bigger's voice died; he was listening to the echoes of his words in his own mind. He saw amaze-

ment and horror on Max's face. Bigger knew that Max would rather not have him talk like this; but he could not help it. He had to die and he had to talk. "Well, it's sort of funny, Mr. Max. I ain't trying to dodge what's coming to me." Bigger was growing hysterical. "I know I'm going to get it. I'm going to die. Well, that's all right now. But really I never wanted to hurt nobody. That's the truth, Mr. Max. I hurt folks 'cause I felt I had to; that's all. They were crowding me too close; they wouldn't give me no room. Lots of times I tried to forget 'em, but I couldn't. They wouldn't let me. . . ." Bigger's eyes were wide and unseeing; his voice rushed on: "Mr. Max I didn't mean to do what I did. I was trying to do something else. But it seems like I never could. I was always wanting something and I was feeling that nobody would let me have it. So I fought 'em. I thought they was hard and I acted hard." He paused, then whimpered in confession, "But I ain't hard, Mr. Max. I ain't hard even a little bit. . . ." He rose to his feet. "But I— I won't be crying none when they take me to that chair. But I'll b-b-be feeling inside of me like I was crying. . . . I'll be feeling and thinking that they didn't see me and I didn't see them. . . ." (355)

Bigger understands and articulates quite coherently what he is and how he became what he is. Bigger's spiritual awakening now complete, we no longer need the narrator to intermediate, to bridge the gap between Bigger's turbulent consciousness and our perception of that consciousness. The rebelliousness, the pride, the volatile temperament, and the fear are superseded by a new depth that embodies self-knowledge and spiritual growth.

Having found hope within himself, Bigger takes emotional responsibility for himself, forcing his reality upon the worn and resigned Max. Moreover, the narrator, who previously guided the reader through the flux and flow of Bigger's consciousness in Books 1 and 2, and the initial parts of Book 3, becomes less obtrusive. Wright interweaves dramatic dialogue with the interpretive voice of the narrator to accentuate Bigger's ability to express the depths of his own thoughts. The reader, then, is able to separate Bigger's consciousness from the voice of the narrator. Instead of serving their usual role as translators of Bigger's thoughts, the narrator's comments function as asides or stage directions. From this point on, the narrator virtually disappears and the novel progresses to its end through dramatic dialogue between Max and Bigger.

Bigger emerges from his ordeal as a composite, individual personality whose tragic fate arouses our compassion as well as our alarm. We do not forget that while external forces always set the tragic pattern into action, the hero himself is in part responsible for his fate. Bigger, too, realizes this as his "faint, wry, bitter smile" follows Max down the steel corridors when Max leaves him to his impending death. This understanding of his role in his fate and of the emotional liaison that binds all of humanity make Bigger a universal hero, pulling him out of the mire of naturalism into the realm of tragedy. Through the magnitude of his suffering and through his perception of it, Bigger joins a host of protagonists whose suffering Sewall cites as tragic. In reference to the protagonists of *The Scarlet Letter*, *Moby-Dick*, and *The Brothers Karamazov*, Sewall writes, "That these people achieve tragic stature—anything but 'little'—is due in large part to their capacities, developed through suffering, to understand themselves, judge themselves, and see in their lot an image of the universal" (148).

4. Technique: The Figurative Web

The crux of tragedy is ambiguity in the characterization of the hero and irony embodied in the events that affect the hero's life. Richard Wright's *Native Son* epitomizes this duality in the personality of Bigger Thomas. With Bigger's consciousness at the center of the novel, Wright creates the mood of exploration and anxiety (Sewall 25) through his portrayal of Bigger as paradoxically indifferent and violent, fearful and prideful, sullen and passionate. As shown in Chapter 3, the narrator, identified with Bigger's consciousness, ensures that we perceive simultaneously Bigger's vulnerability and his violent temperament. Thus the narrator's guidance along with the ambiguity in Bigger's character explains why it is possible not only to feel sympathy for but also to like Bigger Thomas, who is both murderer and hero. Yet, the sublimity of the novel lies in the connection between Wright's characterization of Bigger and his unique use of sentence structure and figurative language. For *Native Son* is a linguistically complex network of sentences and images that reflect the opposing or contradictory aspects of Bigger's psyche and thus synthesize the interrelationship between Wright's subject matter and his expression of it.

Much of the criticism on *Native Son* has focused too exclusively on the image of the snow and the metaphor of blindness. It has overlooked the tightly knit web which Wright creates through his figurative use of the colors black, white, and yellow and the interrelationship between the images of the snow, the sun, the wall (the "white looming mountain"), the metaphor of blindness, and

Wright's sentence patterns. (For individual discussions of the metaphors of blindness and the snow, see Baron 17–28, Kinnamon 135–37, Rickels 12, Margolies 117.) Similarly, naturalistic and existential views of Bigger as either a victimized or isolated figure limit the dimensions of Bigger's character and give no attention to how Wright's use of language punctuates the irony and ambiguity of Bigger's personality. Irony in Bigger's characterization, in the sequence of events that affect his life, and in the language is the foundation upon which Wright builds his tragic theme. The fact that Bigger is at once separate from others (that is, individual) and at the same time connected to them (that is, universal) parallels the ambiguous, interlocked symbols of the snow, the sun, and the wall, and the colors white, yellow, and black. For as is the case with the elements of Bigger's personality, these symbols have contrapuntal meanings that parallel and, at the same time, contrast with each other.

When Wright says that the rhythms of Bigger's life vacillate between "indifference and violence; periods of abstract brooding and periods of intense desire; moments of silence and moments of anger," he himself links the ambiguity of Bigger's personality to the language he uses to depict that personality. The periodic, balanced, and compound sentences in the novel unite with the symbols to supplement Wright's theme. (For a prior reading of the sentence patterns and the colors black, white, and yellow, see Joyce, "Style and Meaning" 112–15.) Just as the colors black, white, and yellow, blindness, snow, the sun, and the wall all achieve symbolic depth as representations of Bigger's ambiguous character, the rhythm of many sentences highlights the discrepancy between Bigger's perception of himself and the view of him held by others. Hence the figurative language and the rhetorical function of the sentences coalesce as integral embodiments of Wright's single purpose—to depict the nature of truth through his characterization of Bigger Thomas. For the ironic nature of Bigger's psyche, of the events that affect his life, and of the language that describes him exemplify the dialectic of the tragic form described by Sewall: "It [the tragic form] is a way . . . of making an important—and 'tragic'—statement about the nature of truth. In tragedy, truth is not revealed as one harmonious whole; it is many-faceted, ambiguous, a sum of irreconcilables—and that is one source of its terror" (13).

The periodic sentences which summarize past events, introduce Bigger's state of mind, and justify his actions both alleviate the intensity of the terror evoked by Bigger's harsh actions and emphasize the changes in his state of mind at different intervals. In Book 3, when Bigger is first confined, Wright uses a series of participial phrases to describe the hope and rebelliousness which motivated Bigger in Books 1 and 2:

> Having been thrown by an accidental murder into a position where he had sensed a possible order and meaning in his relations with the people about him; having accepted the moral guilt and responsibility for that murder because it made him feel free for the first time in his life; having felt in his heart some obscure need to be at home with people and having demanded ransom money to enable him to do it—having done all this and failed, he chose not to struggle any more. (234)

These earlier feelings are juxtaposed to the new and more dominant feelings of resignation and helplessness stated succinctly in the final independent clause. A manipulative tool of the third-person limited narrator, this periodic sentence does far more than assure the reader's perception of the sudden changes in nuances that have taken place in Bigger's consciousness. It illuminates that complex ability of the human psyche to hold conflicting feelings simultaneously as it analyzes them and discards those that fail to be beneficial.

Not only do the periodic sentences reveal the contrasts within Bigger's own consciousness; they also exemplify the irreconcilable differences between Bigger's attitude and that of his family toward his rebelliousness. Interpreting Bigger's response to the shame and humiliation on the faces of his family as they visit him in jail, the narrator explains: "While looking at his brother and sister and feeling his mother's arms about him; while knowing that Jack and G. H. and Gus were standing awkwardly in the doorway staring at him in curious disbelief—while being conscious of all this, Bigger felt a wild outlandish conviction surge in him: *They ought to be glad!*" (252). This series of elliptical clauses stresses the emotional chasm that separates Bigger from all others in his Black environment. Moreover, these clauses illustrate a perfect balance between form and meaning. For just as the elliptical clauses depend on the independent clause to complete their meaning, it is in this scene that Bigger, upon hearing of the assaults upon his family, begins to perceive the relationship between his actions and the well-being of his family. Thus the periodic sentence suggests the simultaneity of irreconcilable opposites: Bigger's alienation from others as well as his connection to something outside himself.

The balanced and compound sentences prove to be even more illuminative of this paradox. In the scene in which Bigger succumbs to Buckley's coercion and signs a confession, Wright uses a balanced sentence which juxtaposes Bigger's physical helplessness to his emotional strength:

> He lay on the cold floor sobbing; but really he was standing up strongly with contrite heart, holding his life in his hands, staring at it with a wondering question. He lay on the cold floor sobbing; but really he was pushing forward with his puny strength against a world too big and too strong for him. He lay on the cold floor sobbing; but really he was groping forward with fierce zeal into a welter of circumstances which he felt contained a water of mercy for the thirst of his heart and brain. (264)

Here, contrasting ideas occur within the same grammatical structure. The repeated independent clause which emphasizes Bigger's intense despair contrasts with the varying independent clauses which describe the hope Bigger feels despite the severity of his circumstances. No other group of sentences more aptly illustrates the paradoxical nature of Bigger's personality. Whereas the Bigger of

Books 1 and 2 is simultaneously fearful and prideful, indifferent and violent, the Bigger of Book 3 is at once physically impotent and emotionally resolute.

As is the case with Bigger's personality, irreconcilable opposites also underlie the harsh realities of racially and socially segregated communities in *Native Son*. Achieving a superb balance between form and content, Wright uses the compound sentence to stress the power whites have over Blacks as well as the aberrations engendered in both by stereotypes based on class and sex. The compound sentence accompanies the metaphorical function of the colors black and white in their representation of the social, economic, and political forces that govern Bigger's life. These elements of language manifest the cosmological order that divides society into groups—Black and white, rich and poor, male and female.

The series of compound sentences which describes Bigger's immediate thoughts concerning his murder of Mary accentuates the overwhelming severity of the codes controlling the interaction between the Black and white worlds in the novel: "He stood with her body in his arms in the silent room and cold facts battered him like waves sweeping in from the sea; she was dead; she was white; she was a woman; he had killed her; he was black; he might be caught; he did not want to be caught; if he were they would kill him" (77). Whereas the balanced and periodic sentences discussed above focus on the paradoxical elements within Bigger's psyche, the compound sentence highlights the incongruity between Bigger's world view and that of the white world. The simile comparing the "cold facts" of Bigger's thoughts to "waves sweeping in from the sea" suggests, as does Wright's use of setting, that the forces of the white world are as powerful and as invincible as those of the natural environment.

But the apparent invincibility of the white world in *Native Son* is underlaid with frailties. Bigger escapes immediate detection as Mary's murderer only because the Daltons and the rest of the whites who question him fail to see the full scope of his humanity. A series of stark compound sentences describing Bigger's response to Mrs. Dalton's questioning shows how her stereotyped notions of race, class, and sex render her psychologically ineffective in communicating with Bigger and in seeing through his mask of humility: "She must know this house like a book, he thought. He trembled with excitement. She was white and he was black; she was rich and he was poor; she was old and he was young; she was the boss and he was the worker. He was safe; yes" (109). Perfect examples of the irony that is the essential element holding all parts of the novel together, this series of compound sentences and the use of polysyndeton explicitly place racial, class, and age categories in equal grammatical structures while their implicit message is a condemnation of the injustices that arise from these categories.

Wright's ingenious use of periodic, balanced, and compound sentences is only part of the intricate language system through which Bigger's tragic fate evolves. Complementing Bigger's ambiguous characterization and the ironic events that shape his destiny are the interconnections among the rhythmic sentence patterns; the colors black, white, and yellow; the images of the wall, the sun, and the snow; and the metaphor of blindness. In their figurative function, the wall and the color black unite with the balanced sentence in their portrayal of Bigger's helplessness and physical impotence. Suggestive of the entrapment described in the balanced sentence, black represents the fear and humiliation Bigger feels in the face of the white world. Upon Bigger's initial visit to the Dalton home, the fear and shame he feels in the presence of whites are so intense that he remains on the verge of hysteria during the entire interview with Mr. Dalton. Thus when Bigger first meets Mr. Dalton, the word *black* accentuates the psychological chasm that separates the two men: "Grabbing the arms of the chair, he pulled himself upright and found a tall, lean, white-haired man holding a piece of paper in his hand. The man was gazing at him with an amused smile that made him conscious of every square inch of skin on his *black* body" (39, emphasis mine). Mr. Dalton's "amused smile" reflects the superiority, power, and emotional distance characteristic of a representative from the godlike world that controls Bigger's life. It is no accident that this white-haired man holds a (white) piece of paper. These symbols are markers for the subjugation that causes Bigger to recoil in acute awareness of his blackness. Consequently, Wright's use of *black* interacts with setting. For just as Mr. Dalton is identified with the power and stability cultivated by his environment, Bigger's encounter with that environment produces feelings of inferiority and entrapment.

Although the word *black* appears throughout the novel, two other passages make especially vivid its metaphorical dimensions. The first occurs in the scene in which Bigger murders Bessie. Despite the fact that Bessie coerces Bigger into confiding in her, once she learns of the magnitude of his crime she desperately wants to retreat. Bigger must then keep her with him until he realizes that her extreme fear will only accelerate his capture. Soon after he decides that he has to kill her, they step into a deserted building to rest. Wright uses *black* three times in this single passage to underscore Bessie's despair and impotence:

> He [Bigger] put his shoulder to it [the door] and gave a stout shove; it yielded grudgingly. It was *black* inside and the feeble glow of the flashlight did not help much. . . . He circled the spot of the flashlight; the floor was carpeted with *black* dirt and he saw two bricks lying in corners. He looked at Bessie; her hands covered her face and he could see the damp of tears on her *black* fingers. (196, emphasis mine)

Black in this passage connects with Wright's use of setting to reflect Bigger's growing feelings of entrapment and fear. It also suggests that Bessie's cowering and feelings of remorse stem from her humiliation at her blackness as well as her fear of the white world.

The other scene in which *black* is used with especially strong significance occurs during Rev. Hammond's visit with Bigger in jail in Book 3. Rev. Hammond epitomizes the Black community's acceptance of the guilt and shame that arise from their blackness.

Bigger intuitively associates the newspapers' descriptions of him as brutish, ignorant, and inferior with Rev. Hammond's passivity and penitence:

> He [Bigger] stared at the man's jet-*black* suit and remembered who he was. . . . And at once he was on guard against the man. . . . He feared that the preacher would make him feel remorseful. He wanted to tell him to go; but so closely associated in his mind was the man with his mother and what she stood for that he could not speak. In his feelings he could not tell the difference between what this man evoked in him and what he read in the papers. . . . (240, emphasis mine)

Here *black* is the touchstone for Bigger's response to Rev. Hammond, his Job-like rejection of this counselor's religious palaver. The use of the word *black* appears to be inadvertent in the one-line paragraph after Rev. Hammond's prayer for Bigger: "Bigger's black face rested in his hands and he did not move" (243). Actually, *black* functions here as the symbolic finale of the suffering, shame, and penitence expressed in the prayer. When Bigger eventually pulls the preacher's cross from around his neck, he demonstrates his final rejection of the humiliation linked to his blackness.

A traditional metaphor for impotence and resistance (Cirlot 343), the image of the wall accompanies *black* and Wright's use of setting to reflect his character's state of mind by representing limiting situations or obstructions that challenge Bigger. Wright's rhythmic use of the image of the wall satisfies T. R. Henn's description of what he refers to as dominant images in his discussion of those characteristic of the tragic structure. A dominant image is "one or more images that, by specific statement or inference, provide a framework or theme for the play; and in terms of which part or all of the dramatic statement is made. These will be of varying degrees of subtlety . . ." (135). Of more than twenty-nine instances in which Wright depicts Bigger or Bessie physically backed against a wall, the two most powerful scenes, filled with persistent references to wall, both take place in the basement of the Dalton home.

In both scenes the basement and the furnace containing Mary's burning body unite as the focus of the ultimate tests that confront Wright's hero. In addition to the fact that the basement becomes the gathering place for the newspaper reporters and Britten, Mr. Dalton's private detective, the droning furnace also serves as a constant reminder of Bigger's vulnerability. Dominating these scenes, the walls of the basement surrounding Bigger emphasize the extent of his entrapment and the severity of his physical impotence. After he has burned Mary's body and chosen to remain in the Dalton home, his first major challenge is to withstand Britten's hostility and to delude him as he has the Daltons. As Britten questions him, Bigger ponders on the furnace: "The fire sang in Bigger's ears and he saw the red shadows dance on the walls" (133). The more Britten confronts Bigger, the more Bigger thinks of the furnace and meets Britten's challenges with his mask of pusillanimity. When Britten finally thinks he has successfully identified Bigger as a Communist, the wall exemplifies the threatening power of the white world and Bigger's concomitant physical helplessness: "Britten followed Bigger till Bigger's head struck the wall. Bigger looked squarely into his eyes. Britten, with a movement so fast that Bigger did not see it, grabbed him in the collar and rammed his head hard against the wall" (137). Literally backing Bigger up against the wall, Britten, like a god, epitomizes the insensitivity and overwhelming authority of the white world.

Wright concentrates references to the wall in those sections where the power of the white world is most intense in its threat to Bigger. In the climactic scenes that begin with Peggy's discovery of the kidnap note and end with her telling Bigger to clean the furnace, the narrator points out seven times that Bigger stands or leans against a wall. As soon as Bigger plants the kidnap note at the Daltons' front door, he shrewdly joins the reporters and Britten in the basement. The reporters' excitement over the kidnap note spurs a new series of flashing cameras which increases the inevitability of Bigger's fate. Moreover, it is in this scene that Wright's rhythmic use of the furnace coalesces with the image of the wall. Bigger's constant thoughts of the furnace, his failure to clean it before the ashes back up, and the failure of the furnace to warm the house all function as associative elements of the image of the wall, finally resolving into a physical and metaphoric trap.

Thus the reporter's taking the shovel and Bigger's fleeing for his life as all the reporters stand amazed at what they believe to be Mary's bones are the natural results of the physical setting represented by the wall. R. E. Baldwin sums up nicely how the recurring image of the wall reflects Bigger's powerlessness and impotence. Describing the progression of the novel, Baldwin says:

> The general outlines of development can be sketched by tracing the rich imagery of rooms, walls, curtains, and other forms of isolation, enclosure, and definition of social groupings. The basic element of this imagery is the single room; both as a feature of physical setting and as a metaphoric formulation in Bigger's mind, the single room merges with thematic issues to provide a manageable summary of Wright's basic views. (387)

An essential element of Wright's "basic views" is the emotional impotence characteristic of the parties on either side of the wall that segregates a community by race. Adapting the traditional polemic of *black* and *white*, Wright uses the color white to represent the obstructions which deny Bigger's humanity and black (and its associated image of the wall) to signal Bigger's entrapment and physical impotence. Striking image patterns therefore collaborate with Bigger's characterization to express the tragic theme. For just as Bigger's personality embodies irreconcilable opposites, the colors black and white and their associated images manifest the paradoxical experiences that reinforce the tragic plot. While the context of certain passages throughout the novel quantifies and qualifies the meaning of a particular image, the individual meanings are heightened by their interrelationship and interdependence.

While the color black clearly exemplifies Bigger's physical relationship to the white world, white further strengthens Wright's portrayal of Bigger's dilemma by underscoring the moral disorder

of the powerful white world. The color white also appears rhythmically throughout the novel, heightening Wright's depiction of
the shallowness and insensitivity of the world which controls
Bigger's life. Bigger's home environment and his extreme self-
consciousness about his blackness, and the Daltons' wealthy community and their self-assurance, reflect two mutually exclusive
worlds with diametrically opposed world views. A look at the description of the Daltons' neighborhood reveals how the color white
symbolizes the emotional distance and economic power of the
white world:

> But while walking through this quiet and spacious *white*
> neighborhood, he did not feel the pull and mystery of the
> thing as strongly as he had in the movie. The houses he passed
> were huge; lights glowed softly in windows. The streets were
> empty, save for an occasional car that zoomed past on swift
> rubber tires. This was a cold and distant world; a world of
> *white* secrets carefully guarded. He could feel a pride, a cer-
> tainty, and a confidence in these streets and houses. . . . All he
> had felt in the movie was gone; only fear and emptiness filled
> him now. (37–38, emphasis mine)

Of all the references to whiteness, this one describing Bigger's
entrance into the white world emerges as the most important
because it stresses how environmental differences account for psychological ones. The reality of the Daltons' white world rekindles
Bigger's sense of helplessness, for their environment is an integral
element of their overwhelming power.

The interrelationship between Wright's use of *white* to represent
the white world's authority and hostility and the image of the wall
to suggest Bigger's impotence when confronted by the white world
shows how the image clusters in *Native Son* collaborate or inter-
lock with each other as expressions of the tragic theme. Interestingly enough, in the scene in which Bigger is forced to visit his
family under the watchful eyes of Jan, Max, the Daltons, and Buckley, it is these whites who the narrator consistently says are stand-

ing along the wall. Exercising their control of Bigger's destiny and
his family's, these representatives of the white world insensitively
deny them the privacy that would spare them their shame. The
wall highlights the aloofness and the abuse of authority that typify
the actions of the white characters in the novel. Unavoidably
aware of the staring white faces, Bigger struggles to redress the lie
he has just told his mother: "Yes; he had to wipe out that lie
[Bigger has told his mother that he will be out of jail in no time],
not only so that they might know the truth, but to redeem himself
in the eyes of those *white* faces behind his back along the *white
wall*. . . . he would not lie, not in the presence of that *white mountain looming* behind him" (253, emphasis mine). The "white looming mountain," with its suggestions of both muteness and mas-
siveness, symbolizes at once the psychological limitations as well
as the political and economic power of those whites who watch
Bigger and his family.

In the same way that *black*, the metaphor of the wall, and the
"white looming mountain" are connected, *white* and the metaphor
of blindness merge as associative figurative patterns evoking shallowness and a lack of perception. The description of Mrs. Dalton
and of her actual physical blindness demonstrates the link between
Wright's use of *white* and blindness. The narrator uses the same
terms to describe Mrs. Dalton throughout the novel as he does
when Bigger first meets her: ". . . he saw coming slowly toward
him a tall, thin, white woman, walking silently, her hands lifted
delicately in the air and touching the walls to either side of her. . . .
Her face and hair were completely white; she seemed to him like a
ghost" (40). In the murder scene, when Mrs. Dalton enters the bed-
room as Bigger leans over Mary, the narrator says, "A white blur
was standing by the door, silent, ghostlike" (73). The consistent
descriptions of Mrs. Dalton as a "white blur" and a "ghostlike figure" suggest the insubstantiality of her philanthropic ideology.
Like her daughter, she does not understand that the social, political, and economic elements of the different environments which
nurture her and Bigger instill in them totally different psychologi-

cal responses to the world around them and forbid their having a
meaningful relationship.

The language she and her husband use in discussing Bigger as
they consider his future reflects their emotional distance and their
mechanical treatment of him. Responding to her husband's hesi-
tancy to encourage Bigger to go back to school, Mrs. Dalton says,
"I think it's important emotionally that he feels free to trust his
environment. . . . Using the analysis contained in the case record
the relief sent us, I think we should evoke an immediate feeling of
confidence . . ." (40). Mrs. Dalton's "strange words" evidence that
she does not feel for Bigger as a fellow human being, a point made
earlier in Chapter 2. Although her conception of herself as superior
is so ingrained into her psyche that she is not aware of it, her natural manner of speaking reveals it at every turn. And when Max
questions Mr. Dalton during Bigger's trial, the hypocrisy and blindness that characterize the Daltons' attitude toward Bigger is explicitly revealed. For Max has Mr. Dalton confess that he does not
think it proper to employ Blacks in his real estate offices, and that
he does not think it proper to lease apartments to Blacks in white
neighborhoods. Blindly, then, the Daltons believe that they improve the quality of life for Blacks by hiring them in menial posi-
tions and by donating thousands of dollars to keep young Black
men entertained at recreation centers. Hence what superficially
looks like naivete is the Daltons' insensitivity to Bigger's plight.
Their viewing him as a fellow human being would demand that
they relinquish their roles as superior, godlike beings and give Bigger equal status among them and their kind. This stance of superiority, lodged deeply and immovably in the white unconscious, lies
at the root of the Daltons' blindness as well as Britten's and Buckley's hostility toward Bigger.

Consequently, in the tradition of the great tragedians before
him, Wright uses the metaphor of blindness to reveal a lack of insight in his characters. As is the case with Oedipus and King Lear,
Bigger too suffers from the blindness rooted in his own lack of
self-knowledge, and this reinforces the tragic drama. The irony

inherent in the relationship among Tiresias, the blind seer, and
Oedipus, who physically blinds himself when he gains insight, and
Gloucester, whose eyes are stamped out because he did not see his
son's treachery, is the prototype of Bigger's gain of insight from his
inadvertent act of murder and from the brutality necessitated by
his trying to conceal it. Just as blindness and suffering ultimately
liberate these characters of classical tragedy, so is Bigger brought to
enlightenment by the horrors which materialize from the darkness
of his self-ignorance.

The passage in which Bigger scrutinizes his new vision of his relationship to the white world captures the essence of this metaphoric, many-faceted blindness:

> No, he did not have to hide behind a wall or a curtain now; he
> had a safer way of being safe, an easier way. What he had done
> last night had proved that. Jan was blind. Mary had been blind.
> Mr. Dalton was blind. And Mrs. Dalton was blind; yes, blind
> in more ways than one. . . . She had thought that Mary was
> drunk, because she was used to Mary's coming home drunk.
> And Mrs. Dalton had not known that he was in the room
> with her; it would have been the last thing she would have
> thought of. He was black and would not have figured in her
> thoughts on such an occasion. Bigger felt that a lot of people
> were like Mrs. Dalton, blind. . . . (91)

What Bigger perceives is how "manipulating appearances is really
a way of inducing blindness" (Heilman, *Magic in the Web* 58). Because he understands the way in which "values determine how one
sees" (Heilman, *This Great Stage* 25), he is able, for some time, to
deceive the white world by exploiting its stereotypical notions of
his blackness.

Madness, interwoven with blindness, is another attribute that
Bigger shares with classical tragic heroes. A monumental study already alluded to above, Robert B. Heilman's *This Great Stage: Image and Structure in King Lear*, makes a distinction between that
play's pattern of sight and madness which can also be applied to

the function of the trancelike, phantasmagoric state that often
overwhelms Bigger:

> . . . the sight pattern tends to take man at the level of the *rec-ognition and identification of phenomena*, that of immediate
> practical decision. . . . The madness pattern, however, is con-cerned with the ways in which men *interpret phenomena*, the
> meanings which they find in experience, the general truths
> which they consciously formulate or in terms of which they
> characteristically act, the kind of wisdom, or sophistication,
> which they achieve. What men see and what men believe, of
> course, are intimately related. . . . (*This Great Stage* 180)

On the level of identification of phenomena, Bigger (before his
murder of Mary) and the other characters in *Native Son*—like Lear
and Gloucester—all "miss the point of what is going on around
them" (*This Great Stage* 180). Moreover, until Bigger is shocked
out of his blindness, his mind is incapable of interpreting his expe-riences in a manner that would enable him to learn from them and
exert better control over his life. Therefore, when confronted by
the white world, he panics and slips into a trance.

This trance or phantasmagoric hysteria is equivalent to Lear's
madness. Although descriptions of Bigger's dreamlike state perme-ate Books 1 and 2, the murder scene most acutely illustrates the
intensity of Bigger's trance, which reflects his inability to grasp the
complexity of his experiences. The "madness" begins when he is
forced to carry Mary's body up the stairs to her room: "He felt
strange, possessed, or as if he were acting upon a stage in front of a
crowd of people" (72). Bigger's trancelike state, induced by the ex-treme fear that causes him to lose control, demonstrates his in-ability to sustain contact with reality, as evidenced by the splitting
of his consciousness into two distinct selves. Later in the same
scene when Mrs. Dalton enters Mary's room, "a hysterical terror
seized him, as though he were falling from a great height in a
dream" (73). Because Bigger lacks self-knowledge and an insight
into the pattern of his encounter with the white world, he blindly
succumbs to his own vulnerability.

The obvious, reasonable solutions to his dilemma never occur to him because he fears the white world so intensely. Hence, instead of summoning Mary's parents or leaving her in the basement in her drunken condition, he carries her up the stairs to her room, accelerating, like Oedipus, his own tragic fate. As discussed in Chapter 3, after being completely seized with terror and killing Mary by pressing the pillow too tightly over her face, he finally realizes that, for some time, he had lost total contact with the world around him: "Gradually, the intensity of his sensations subsided and he was aware of the room. He felt that he had been in the grip of a weird spell and was now free. The fingertips of his right hand were pressed deeply into the soft fibers of the rug and his whole body vibrated from the wild pounding of his heart" (75). The "weird spell" resulting from Bigger's fear is the direct cause of Mary's death.

Characteristic of the paradoxes indigenous to tragedy, Bigger's trancelike condition ironically propels him into rebelliousness which manifests the chaos of his world. The blindness and the trance merge as expressions of the total breakdown of natural order that Wright describes in *Native Son*. The novel presents a world divided into groups, with one group having complete dominance over the other. Wright's point is that this imposition of hierarchy where none should exist is a "breach of nature" that has at its source nothing less than the problem of evil itself (Heilman, *This Great Stage* 174). Consequently, all parts of *Native Son*—its title, Bigger's characterization, his being thrust deeper into his fate, his fear, and the elements of language—collaborate as integral elements of a cosmological order in which nothing is as it should be. In this world where irony is the controlling principle and distortion of natural order a given fact, an act of murder gives Bigger sight and fear emboldens him. Clearly, the young outraged college student, thrown into Bigger's cell because he has gone completely mad over problems of racial injustice, functions as foil to Bigger, suggesting another extreme reaction to the breakdown of natural order that besets their world.

Snow is another dominant image in *Native Son*, joining the

color white and the metaphor of blindness to form an image group
that evokes the hostility, insensitivity, and lack of perception of
the white world and emphasizing the unnatural power the white
world holds over the Black. The white color of snow is caused by
the complete reflection of sunlight from the frozen water crystals;
this reflection is often intense and blinding to the eyes. Hence in
this single image Wright makes final the connection among the
negative attributes of the others. Just as whiteness and blindness
connote animosity and shallowness, the ambivalent snow—a traditional image of danger and destruction—symbolizes the malevolence of the white world and by implication identifies Bigger's
animal-like will to survive.

Although the snow is more than a symbol of white hostility
because of its function as the external counterpart of Bigger's rebellion, traditional criticism on the novel has seen the snow only as a
"persistent symbol of white hostility" (Kinnamon 136). But because
the snow surrounds, impedes, and betrays Bigger as he flees for his
life and because he must fight against it to survive, this image
evokes his defiance at the same time that it represents the animosity of the white world. A superb craftsman, Wright is consistent in his habit of concentrating images in those scenes where the
hero faces the greatest challenges. Snow dominates Book 2, which
begins with Bigger's deception of the white world and ends with
his inevitable capture. The last forty-two pages of Book 2, which
encompass events from the discovery of Mary's bones to Bigger's
capture, contain no fewer than sixty-one references to snow. Although it snows during all of Book 2, the figurative function of
snow increases in impact as Bigger flees for his life. Nine references to snow pervade the single paragraph that describes Bigger's
escape after the reporter takes the shovel from him. Tiptoeing up
the stairs of the basement to his room and lifting the window,

> . . . he felt a cold rush of air laden with snow. . . . He groped
> to the window and climbed into it, feeling again the chil-
> ling blast of snowy wind. . . . he looked into the snow and
> tried to see the ground below. . . . His eyes were shut and his

> hands were clenched as his body turned, sailing through the
> snow. . . . he lay buried in a cold pile of snow, dazed. Snow
> was in his mouth, eyes, ears: snow was seeping down his
> back. . . . He had not been able to control the muscles of his
> hot body against the chilled assault of the wet snow over all
> his skin. . . . he struggled against the snow, pushing it away
> from him. (187)

Because the white world is now able to identify Bigger as Mary's
murderer, the threatening power it has over him will become even
more hostile. This malevolence—beastlike in its force—is suggested by the rhythmic repetition of the word *snow.*

As Bigger flees through the streets of Chicago, he fights his way
through the driving snow, which has fallen quite heavily, encum-
bering traffic and thus increasing in its force. The danger and hostility symbolized by the snow merge with whiteness—its associative metaphor—in the scene which warns that the vigilantes
have almost surrounded the hero. As Bigger looks through the
newspaper, searching the maps for the location of the mob, the
narrator explains: "There was another map of the South Side. This
time the shaded area [showing where the mob was] had deepened
from both the north and south, leaving a small square of white in
the middle of the oblong Black Belt. He stood looking at that tiny
square of white as though gazing down into the barrel of a gun"
(216). The "small square of white" in the map echoes the white
piece of paper Mr. Dalton held earlier in his hand. Instead of cowering and giving in to his fear as he had in his initial visit to Mr.
Dalton's home, Bigger chooses to fight to the end.

His physical journey ends, soon afterwards, on the roof of a tenement building near "a white looming bulk." Fighting instinctively,
Bigger uses the barrel of his gun to knock unconscious the first of
the men who discover him on the roof. The snow warns, however,
that the mob will overpower Bigger's courage. As he slides about
over the roof, "he felt snow in his face and eyes" (222). And finally,
when the mob spots him and fires its first shot, he comes to the
huge, white, snow-covered obstruction, a point at which all the

important figurative elements of the novel up to now—the colors black and white, the wall, and snow—suddenly unite. The multiplicity of this image evidences what Heilman sees as characteristic of life itself. In discussing the image patterns in *King Lear*, he writes, "Nearly every pattern has its dichotomy, and the dichotomies tend to coincide and even coalesce into a general definition of reality" (*This Great Stage* 178). Analogously, the humiliation and fear Bigger feels because of his black skin, the social, economic, political, and psychological limitations imposed by the wall of segregation, the hostility and power of the white world, and the limitations of sight and comprehension all coalesce in the "white looming bulk," a huge water tank draped in snow.

Before he reaches the looming bulk, Bigger wonders what it is and whether he will somehow be able to use it to his advantage: "He wove among the chimneys, his feet slipping and sliding over the snow, keeping in mind that white looming bulk which he had glimpsed ahead of him. Was it something that would help him? Could he get upon it, or behind it, and hold them off?" (224). Ironically, the water tank becomes the weapon that makes Bigger's capture final. Once he crawls to the top and hangs on to the tank, the vigilantes—unsuccessful at all other attempts—spray icy water upon him with a hose attached to the tank. His body stiff and frozen, Bigger finally loses his grip, landing on the roof with his face in the snow. His being "dragged across the snow of the roof" and stretched out on the ground later in the snow as if he were about to be crucified suggest the outcome of the abusive power one group holds over another in a world that has chosen oppression and chaos over harmony and natural order.

The complex, often paradoxical nature of the figurative language Wright uses to depict the unnatural cosmological order in *Native Son* perfectly parallels the contradictory, irreconcilable elements of Bigger's personality. At the same time that the colors black and white, the wall, blindness, Bigger's trancelike state, and the snow have their individual symbolic meanings, they also merge into a unified whole as a collective expression of the phenomena that affect Bigger's consciousness. A part of Bigger's consciousness always remains undisclosed to those around him, but he must also be defined—like the rest of us—in terms of his relationship to the world around him. Because Bigger is existentially isolated from his family and friends and at the same time is subject to the influence of the environment, he emerges as a complex human personality whose pride and fear catapult him into a realm of experiences where he willfully challenges the forces that attempt to subdue him.

Reflecting those juxtapositions of opposites that comprise the complexity characteristic of the human psyche, the snow works together with its diametrically opposed image—the sun—to show Bigger as both murderer and hero respectively. In the same way that the snow represents the animosity of the white world and simultaneously identifies Bigger as a menace, the sun shares a relationship with its corresponding color yellow, which evokes both heroism and danger. This final image group completes the tightly interwoven relationship of the figurative constituents in *Native Son*. The sun—the seat of life and energy (Frazer 79)—highlights Bigger as hero while its associated color yellow connects with the color white to prefigure danger.

Although yellow—the attribute of Apollo, the sun-god—traditionally indicates magnanimity, intuition, and intellect (Cirlot 52), it is also coupled with white by its position on an upward-tending color scale in which black and white represent two extremes (Cirlot 51). Yellow light abounds in those scenes where Bigger is quite vulnerable to forces that pursue him, and becomes increasingly forceful as it develops an affinity with the white snow in the final, climactic scene of Book 2. As Bigger darts about on the roof of the tenement buildings, he desperately struggles to avoid the continuous, intense flashes of yellow light from the searchlights the vigilantes use in their pursuit. In the passage in which the first flash of yellow light occurs, the narrator—in his role as interpreting guide—explains that the yellow lights are the inescapable manifestations of Bigger's equally inescapable fate:

His eyes jerked upward as a huge, sharp beam of yellow light
shot into the sky. Another came, crossing it like a knife. Then
another. Soon the sky was full of them. They circled slowly,
hemming him in; bars of light forming a prison, a wall between him and the rest of the world; bars weaving a shifting
wall of light into which he dared not go. He was in the midst
of it now; this was what he had been running from ever since
that night Mrs. Dalton had come into the room and charged
him with such fear that his hands had gripped the pillow with
fingers of steel and had cut off the air from Mary's lungs. (218)

The yellow bars of light are prefigured early in Book 1 by the
red-hot iron that Bigger feels in his throat when he thinks of whites
and of his mother's premonition. Suggesting the magnitude of the
forces that overpower Bigger, yellow now merges with the image of
the wall to become an element of setting. For both these images,
along with the threatening snow, symbolize the effect of the moral,
social, economic, and political laws aimed at stifling Bigger's life.

The sun contrasts with the snow, illuminating Bigger as the hero
determined to maintain his pride and to subvert those forces that
deny his humanity. The use of the sun to counteract negative responses to a rebellious protagonist beautifully evidences Wright's
skill at sustaining a balance between the subjectivity rooted in
the author's identification with his characters and the objectivity
reflected in the artist's superb mastery of his craft. Forming an
affinity with the interpretive, third-person limited narrator, the
sun—symbolic of reflection and willpower (Cirlot 303)—appears
primarily in the scenes where Bigger questions his relationship to
the white world and where his role in his own fate becomes increasingly clear first to the reader and finally to Bigger himself.

The sun pervades Books 1 and 3, presaging Bigger's destiny in the
beginning and heralding his transcendence at the end. In the early
scenes, the sun illuminates the elements in Bigger's environment
and in his personality that later undergird the act of will responsible for his defiance of the established order of the white world. A

scene from Book 1 serves as a good example of this function of the sun. Intensely frustrated because they are hemmed in, forbidden to participate in the mainstream of life, Bigger and Gus hang along the street and listlessly share their fantasies. As they watch an airplane move across the sky, Bigger discloses his wish to fly a plane. When Gus responds with "God'll let you fly when He gives you your wings up in heaven" (15), he is expressing their despair at the extent of the control the white world has over them. The sun image that immediately follows evokes the intensity of Bigger's dissatisfaction with that world's power and foreshadows his imminent rebellion:

> They laughed again, reclining against the wall, smoking, the lids of their eyes drooped softly against the sun. Cars whizzed past on rubber tires. Bigger's face was metallically black in the strong sunlight. There was in his eyes a pensive, brooding amazement, as of a man who had been long confronted and tantalized by a riddle whose answer seemed always just on the verge of escaping him, but prodding him irresistibly on to seek its solution. (15)

The lack of insight and comprehension that characterizes Bigger in Book 1 is also responsible for the constant rifts between him and his gang. Because his overwhelming pride keeps him from acknowledging even to himself his intense fear of whites, he contrives a fight with Gus in a futile attempt to hide his real feelings. Once the fight is over and Bigger has completely severed his relations with his friends, the sun highlights his alienation:

> He shut the knife and slipped it in his pocket and swung the door [of Doc's poolroom] to the street. He blinked his eyes from the bright sunshine; his nerves were so taut that he had difficulty in breathing. . . .
>
> He had an overwhelming desire to be alone; he walked to the middle of the next block and turned into an alley. . . . When he reached the end of the alley, he turned into a street, walking slowly in the sunshine, his hands jammed deep into his pockets, his head down, depressed. (35)

In Book 3 as Bigger lies in his jail cell awaiting his death, the narrator explains that Bigger has stopped responding to any stimuli from the world around him: "Most of the time he sat with bowed head, staring at the floor; or he lay full length upon his stomach, his face buried in the crook of an elbow, just as he lay now upon a cot with the pale yellow sunshine of a February sky falling obliquely upon him through the cold steel bars of the Eleventh Street Police Station" (233). The paleness of the sunshine suggests that, having accepted responsibility for his actions, Bigger feels that he has failed and wants to die. Yet, at the inquest, when Bigger sees that the white world intends to mock him, "to use his death as a bloody symbol of fear to wave before the eyes of the black world" (235), his pride forces him to fight again.

This time the battle takes place exclusively in an emotional arena. Completely entrapped physically by the white world, Bigger must again exercise his newly acquired inner strength and vision. His awakened determination is symbolized by the yellow sunshine that splashes across the sidewalks and buildings outside, where a huge crowd stares at him as he is led from the police station. Instead of taking Bigger directly to the designated Cook County Jail, the police first drive him to the Daltons' home and attempt to have him parody himself by acting out the steps of his crime. Again, the sun shines as the motorcade begins to move through the streets, and when it reaches Drexel Boulevard, the narrator points out that the Daltons' big brick house is completely "drenched in sunshine." Throughout the novel, the sun is directly associated with Bigger, but in this scene Wright uses it ironically. While the Dalton home is of course in mourning, it is drenched in sunlight to symbolize that Mary's death is Bigger's source of life.

In the final scenes of the novel, the sun becomes the reflector of Bigger's spiritual state. To convince the judge to give Bigger a life term in prison rather than sentence him to death, Max feels that his only recourse is to explain to the judge how Bigger sees the world and his relationship to it. Early in Book 3, then, Max engages Bigger in a long discussion that ignites a new kind of fire in Bigger.

For the first time, Bigger begins to lift the veil of hate that had earlier blinded him. Inspired by Max's questions, Bigger experiences new feelings and perceives the connection between his previous feelings and actions. Emphasizing the intensity and depth of Bigger's recognition of a wholeness that binds all people together, Wright has Bigger create his own sun image as a metaphor for his feelings:

> Another impulse rose in him, born of desperate need, and his mind clothed it in an image of a strong blinding sun sending hot rays down and he was standing in the midst of a vast crowd of men, white men and black men and all men, and the sun's rays melted away the many differences, the colors, the clothes, and drew what was common and good upward toward the sun. . . . (307)

This important passage marks the pinnacle of Bigger's revelation.

Bigger now recognizes his affinity with the rest of humanity. Before and especially after his murder of Mary, he felt unconnected to the human world. He was an observer of life, alienated emotionally from his family and friends and denied the social and economic fruits of the American dream he craved intensely. On the eve of his death, he understands that despite the evil effects of racism, we all hold our own value, our own worth within ourselves, and it is this inherent value and our common desires that give each of us a vital place in the scheme of things. The fact that Wright has Bigger imagine his own sun (rather than use the natural sunshine, as he does in all other scenes) punctuates Bigger's final acceptance of his own humanity. For he now understands that although he challenged the white world and attempted to shape his own destiny, he had at the same time internalized the negative image of himself created by that white world.

Bigger's creation of his own sun image attests to his tragic purification and explains the nonvindictiveness that characterizes his acceptance of the judge's refusal of his appeal. He is not surprised to learn that the governor refuses to commute his death sentence to life imprisonment. After receiving the telegram from Max, "he lay down again on the cot, on his back, and stared at the tiny bright-yellow electric bulb glowing in the ceiling above his head. It contained the fire of death" (351). According to T. R. Henn, "Fire is of transcendent value to man. . . . it is given by the gods only as lightning or as the sun . . ." (60). The yellow bulb contains the fire of Bigger's spiritual strength. The light that emanates from the yellow bulb symbolizes the paradox that enfolds *Native Son*. Associated with the sun, which represents spiritual strength and the creative force, yellow here continues to prefigure the threat the white world poses to Bigger. However, having found consolation through the vision entailed in his own sun image, Bigger has attained a spiritual peace that makes him ready to face his death.

5. The Unity of Book 3: A Synthesis of the Theme

The trial, Max's role in Bigger's life, and Max's fourteen-page address to the judge have provoked as much of a critical skirmish as has Bigger's characterization. On one side of the issue are those critics—Irving Howe, Alfred Kazin, Robert Bone, Edward Margolies, Russell Brignano, James Baldwin, Dan McCall, Katherine Fishburn, and Margaret Walker Alexander, for example—who hold that Max's speech is an artistic flaw that merely reflects Communist doctrine. This reading of the address leads to the idea that Book 3 seriously mars the unity of *Native Son* because of Wright's failure to sustain the dramatic action revealed through character rather than commentary. (See Howe 104, Kazin 387, Bone 23, Margolies 113–15, Brignano 81, Baldwin ["Many Thousands Gone"] 18–36, McCall 92, Fishburn 69, Alexander 182–202.) On the other side of the debate, Donald Gibson, Jeffrey Sadler, Paul Siegal, and Edward Kearns all assert that the reader's focus should be not on Max's speech but on Bigger's psychological makeup and the relationship between his development as a character in the first two books and the change he undergoes in the third. (See Gibson ["Wright's Invisible Native Son"] 728–38, Sadler 11–24, Siegal 517–23, Kearns 146–55.) Jeffrey Sadler, moreover, goes one step further when he proposes that instead of being flawed by what some see as Max's obtrusion, Book 3 is an aesthetic success if we read the trial section for what it illuminates about Bigger's character (12). What is important about Max's speech is not its espousal of Communist ideology, nor its length, but rather its affinity with the rest of the novel and, most importantly, the points that make Max's speech an integral embodiment of Wright's characterization of Max and Bigger.

Although Buckley's address to the judge is considerably shorter than Max's, the way previous criticism of Book 3 limits itself to discussions of Max's speech and ignores Buckley's is a serious oversight. This neglect of Buckley's address to the court finds its source in stereotypical conceptions of *Native Son* that fail to see the relationship between the two speeches, to analyze the speeches as extensions of Max's and Buckley's characters, and to perceive the connections between the speeches and the stylistic elements of Books 1 and 2. The most important of the three books, Book 3 embodies and unifies all the salient stylistic constituents—the elements of setting, the role of the narrator, the aspects of Bigger's psyche, and the image patterns—that make up *Native Son*. As is the case with the image patterns and with Bigger's personality, Max's and Buckley's addresses and their respective characterizations reflect irreconcilable opposites important to Wright's delineation of his tragic theme. Rather than being a didactic divergence which "detracts from the sense of unequivocal achievement for *Native Son*" (Brignano 82), the trial section is the dramatic culmination of the breach of nature that affects Bigger's life. Both Max and Buckley represent a world in which an unnatural cosmological order results in the dehumanization typified by a shallowness and callousness of character.

Examples of the synthesis of form which makes Book 3 the natural outcome of the events in Books 1 and 2, Max's and Buckley's speeches echo the threatening implications of Buckley's campaign poster (which is strategically placed in the Black Belt), the power of the white world suggested in Gus and Bigger's game of playing white, Bigger's and his mother's premonitions of his fate, his isolation, his defiant challenge of the stereotypical conceptions of his character, and the imagery which reflects his dilemma. This integration of all the elements that carry the theme of the tragic drama is the final synthesis of the tragic action: ". . . it is the character of the *end* which gives the plot its distinctive quality of a symmetrical narrowing or focusing; and . . . the *end* in its turn is present in the structure, language, and imagery [of the story] . . ." (Henn 20).

Bigger's past converges with his present as he lies on the cot incarcerated at the beginning of Book 3. In spite of Max's long, esoteric address, Book 3 moves quickly as the reader becomes involved in a succession of events: Reverend Hammond visits Bigger in jail; Jan visits him; Buckley interrogates him; his family visits him under the watchful eyes of the Daltons, Jan, Buckley, and Max; Bigger meets Max; Bigger experiences the spectacular inquest and trial; and finally the judge sentences him to death. Neither Bigger, Max, nor the reader is surprised to hear the judge's pronouncement. For at no point during the inquest or the trial is Bigger's fate uncertain. Although he springs back into consciousness to save his pride, his fight becomes a struggle within his own psyche.

After he withstands the humiliation of visiting his family in public view and of succumbing to Buckley by signing a confession, the inquest is the first real event that marks the magnitude of his suffering. While a host of white faces surrounds him, he listens to the testimony of Mrs. Dalton, Jan, and Mr. Dalton as the coroner attempts to convince the jury that he has enough evidence for the state to establish the identity of Mary's body and to convict Bigger as her murderer. The disclosure of Bessie's battered, blood-stained body, Mary's purse, the blood-stained knife, the blackened hatchet blade, the Communist pamphlets, the rum bottle, and the trunk presages the histrionics of the ensuing trial and begins the process in which Bigger is forced to stare at the signs of his horrendous deeds and to contemplate their effect on himself and others. His interaction with Max enhances this new experience of introspection.

Just as we never really imagine Bigger wearing the suit and tie Max sends him, we do not see his growing dependence on Max's physical presence beside him in the courtroom. Entrapped in Bigger's consciousness, we focus, as he himself does, on his determination to grapple with the answers to Max's questions in order to understand the meaning of his life. Of course, when Bigger first meets Max, he is as reluctant to trust him as he is anyone else. But as Max persistently coerces him, the narrator says: "Bigger stared at Max. He felt sorry for the white man. He saw that Max was afraid that he would not talk at all. And he had no desire to hurt Max. . . . Well, tell him. Talk. Get it over with and let Max go" (294). Ironically, Bigger has no way of knowing that the answers to Max's questions during this first long interchange between them will later be reshaped by and infused into Max's Communist ideology to become the nucleus of Max's address to the judge.

The nature of Max's speech and the discrepancy between the speech and his emotional response to Bigger identify Max as a liberal and an idealist who is unable to accept the horrors of life that underlie his own rhetoric. The initial hint of Max's failings is given in the narrator's description of Max when he first meets Bigger. As Jan, who prepares Bigger for Max, leads Max into the room, the narrator says: "He [Bigger] saw a man's head come into the door, a head strange and white, with silver hair and a lean white face that he had never seen before. . . . there was about the man's thin lips a faint smile that seemed to have always been there" (247). By this time in the novel, the reader easily realizes that the color white symbolizes the negative attributes of the white world. Echoing the earlier physical description of Mr. and Mrs. Dalton and Mr. Dalton's "amused smile," Max's white hair and "faint smile" portend that he, too, will respond to Bigger in the same patronizing fashion as the Daltons. As Max's interaction with Bigger progresses, it becomes increasingly clear that he possesses the same shallowness of character as the Daltons, which makes him blind to Bigger's reality.

Max, of course, does not defend Bigger because of a genuine concern for him as an individual human being. When Max encounters Buckley in the room where Bigger is being held, Max reveals his self-serving political purpose for defending Bigger as he accuses Buckley of defaming the Communist party. Because Buckley takes advantage of Bigger's having falsified the Communist insignia on the kidnap note, Max's party compels him to defend Bigger in an attempt to correct the slurs against it and to mitigate the harassment of party members, as well as to advance their cause. In contrast to the plethora of witnesses for the state—Mrs. Dalton, her mother, Britten, fifteen newspapermen, five handwriting specialists, a fingerprint expert, six doctors, four waitresses from Ernie's Kitchen Shack, two white schoolteachers, Jan, the members of Bigger's gang, Doc, and five psychiatrists—Max chooses to be the sole witness for the defense.

In his pretrial statement, Max introduces the ideas on which he later builds his plea to the judge. He urges the judge to remember that the law of the state offers three choices regarding a plea of guilty in a murder case: "the court may impose the death penalty, imprison the defendant for life, or for a term of not less than fourteen years" (319). He explains that this law allows the court the flexibility to consider why a man killed and to use its findings either to aggravate or mitigate the measure of punishment. Pointing out that in its pretrial statement the state has dismissed the issue of why Bigger killed, Max ends his introduction with the ideas that dominate his subsequent address: his tasks will be to elucidate the reasons why Bigger's crimes are "almost instinctive" by nature and to convince the judge that since Bigger's motives are not included in the laws as they are written, he must consider Bigger's mental and emotional makeup before deciding his punishment.

As soon as Max begins his address proper, the reader quickly perceives that such a plea as his will be futile in counteracting the power of the forces that demand Bigger's life. If the nature and length of Max's address frustrate the reader, it is not difficult to imagine the judge's response and that of the others in the courtroom. In contrast to Buckley's well-timed, sensational, vitriolic performance, Max's excessively long speech challenges the intellectual and moral faculties of the observers. In his pretrial statement Buckley quite aptly characterizes Max's speech and presages its effect when he says, "There is no room here for evasive, theoretical, or fanciful interpretations of the law" (316).

Interweaving the image patterns, Bigger's personality, and the elements of setting into the fabric of the speech, Wright has Max give a theoretical interpretation of what it means to be Bigger Thomas. Wright has him echo both the ironic title of the novel and the elements of setting at the very beginning, when Max pronounces that Bigger's destiny is America's destiny. As implied by the title of the novel, Bigger is a creation of an American culture that ironically rejects him and denies his social, economic, and political freedom. This denial, Max avers, has a crippling effect on those who control Bigger's life as well as on Bigger. Max's idea that the white world's life and fate are linked to Bigger's parallels Wright's use of *black* and *white* as well as the images of the snow and the sun. The symbolic meanings of *black* and *white* reflect the contrast in Bigger's and Mary's emotional makeup and underline the relationship that describes their lives. For while the white characters define themselves in relation to the Black, the Blacks in turn depend on the whites for their social, political, and economic livelihood. Also a part of Wright's depiction of this relationship, the snow and the sun represent respectively the white world's power and hostility and Bigger's reaction to that power.

Max's address directly attributes Bigger's rebelliousness and fear to the godlike power the Daltons have over Bigger and his kind. Synonymous with the "white looming mountain" and the image of the wall (see Chapter 4), various sections of Max's speech show how the social and economic barriers that separate the black and white worlds are so great that they have the same power and psychological effect on Bigger as acts of nature. Max says: "When situations like this arise, instead of men feeling that they are facing other men, they feel that they are facing mountains, floods, seas: forces of nature whose size and strength focus the minds and emotions to a degree of tension unusual in the quiet routine of urban life. Yet this tension exists within the limits of urban life, undermining it and supporting it in the same gesture of being" (327).

This tension between the alluring and repellent aspects of urban culture contains a double-barreled irony. Illuminating a part of this irony, Max paints an esoteric picture of the forbidden fruits that taunt Bigger:

Your Honor, consider the mere physical aspect of our civilization. How alluring, how dazzling it is! How it excites the senses! How it seems to dangle within easy reach of everyone the fulfillment of happiness! How constantly and overwhelmingly the advertisements, radios, newspapers and movies play upon us! But in thinking of them remember that to many they are tokens of mockery. . . . Imagine a man walking amid such a scene, a part of it, and yet knowing that it is *not* for him! (332)

Reminiscent of the setting of Books 1 and 2—which contrasts Bigger's thwarted aspirations and the poverty of his home environment with Mary's unfettered lifestyle and the luxuries of her home environment—Max's portrait presents the paradox reflected in the environmental constituents that affect Bigger's consciousness.

An essential thread—perhaps the most important—tying Max's characterization of Bigger to that of the first two books is his reference to Bigger's instinctive, organic reaction to his oppressive environment. The image of Bigger as a suppressed, frightened animal arises throughout the novel and emerges as the focus of Max's defense. This image complements that of the sun by suggesting that the animal nature of human beings is as characteristic a part of the human personality as is the power of reason. Treated like an animal, Bigger naturally cultivates the survival instincts of the prey that engages in battle with its predator. For instance, early in Book 1 when Bigger meets the Daltons for the first time, as he stands with his knees slightly bent, his shoulder stooped, his eyes blank, the narrator uses the word *organic* to explain Bigger's posture: "There was an organic conviction in him that this was the way white folks wanted him to be when in their presence; none had ever told him that in so many words, but their manner had made him feel that they did" (42). Consequently, Bigger instinctively assumes the role that he hopes will protect him while he is in the presence of his enemy.

Max's description of Bigger as an animal both created and caged by the stifling conditions of urban life is a subtle reshaping of Bigger's own attitude toward his resistance. While Bigger reacts as any human being might have under similar circumstances, paradoxically these same actions illuminate him as the hero unable to acquiesce to the status quo that those around him accept. His response to Max's question about the role religion has played in his life encapsulates that aspect of his attitude toward life which makes him distinctive. When Max asks if he could be happy in church, Bigger explains that the church brings only the kind of happiness that white folks want him to have: "If I was religious, I'd be dead now" (302). Religion, Bigger adds, is for "whipped folks." This rejection of the passivity and weakness cultivated by religion and his determination to enjoy the fruits of American culture fuel the rebellious spirit, which Max says is so natural that it "expresses itself, like a weed growing from under a stone" (330).

Through its allusion to Bigger as an organic force, the simile above supplements Max's striking metaphor of Bigger as a beastlike corpse that a guilt-ridden American society attempts to bury. But instead of surrendering to the overwhelming, stifling forces of the white world, the beast retaliates ferociously. Max exclaims:

> For the corpse is not dead! It still lives! It has made itself a home in the wild forest of our great cities, amid the rank and choking vegetation of slums! It has forgotten our language! In order to live it has sharpened its claws! It has grown hard and calloused! It has developed a capacity for hate and fury which we cannot understand! Its movements are unpredictable! By night it creeps from its lair and steals toward the settlements of civilization! And at the sight of a kind face it does not lie down upon its back and kick up its heels playfully to be tickled and stroked. No; it leaps to kill! (331)

Easily the most dramatic part of Max's defense, this image of Bigger as a dangerous beast captures the essence of the irony which undergirds *Native Son*. In order to hide its guilt and fear, white society, according to Max, segregates and oppresses Bigger, attempting to render him docile and harmless. Yet, the effects of this oppression ironically become the motivating forces behind Bigger's destructive actions.

Wright repeats the word *leap* to describe Bigger's actions and feelings almost as often as he does *organic*. The two concepts work together, serving the same function as that described by Heilman for the animal imagery in *King Lear*: "The animal imagery, which is plentiful, is used almost exclusively to emphasize another complication in humanity—its capacity for abjuring its especial characteristics and taking on the rapacity and ruthlessness of the beast . . ." (*This Great Stage* 176). Max's ending his description of the beast with "it leaps to kill" brings to a crescendo the rhythmic chord that accentuates the instinctive, ruthless nature of Bigger's fear throughout the novel. Whenever Bigger feels embarrassed, trapped, or threatened by the white world or by a suggestion of the power that world holds, Wright uses *leap* to describe the intensity of Bigger's fear and of his innate proclivity for survival. For example, quite early in Book 1, when Mary unknowingly humiliates Bigger by suggesting that he join her and Jan in Ernie's Kitchen Shack, the narrator says, "Mary asked in a sweet tone that made him want to *leap* at her" (61, emphasis mine). And later, when Buddy follows Bigger outside to give him the roll of bills that had fallen from his pockets, "Bigger looked at him, his body as taut as that of an animal about to *leap*" (94, emphasis mine). His mother, of course, embarrasses him almost insufferably when she falls to her knees before Mr. and Mrs. Dalton: "Bigger's shame for his mother amounted to hate. He stood with clenched fists, his eyes burning. He felt that in another moment he would have *leaped* at her" (257, emphasis mine).

Thus any abuse that challenges Bigger's strong sense of pride induces in him an almost uncontrollable desire to destroy the source of his distress. For the most part throughout Book 3, he maintains a calm and resigned demeanor. But when Max asks during their initial session if he liked Mary, Bigger becomes nearly as hysterical as he was during his fight with Gus in Doc's poolroom: "Bigger's voice boomed so suddenly from his throat that Max started. Bigger *leaped* to his feet; his eyes widened and his hands lifted midway to his face, trembling" (296, emphasis mine). Bigger's intense response to Max's inquiry into his feeling for Mary evinces that Mary epitomizes those collective forces that humiliate and threaten him.

Bigger's hatred for Mary, Max contends, stems from the same environmental conditions as Mary's and her parents' condescension. Max struggles to outline the cause of the emotional chasm that separates Bigger and Mary. In doing so, he makes a connection between the metaphor of blindness and Bigger's ironic, organic rebellion. He asks the court:

> Do you think that you can kill one of them—even if you killed one every day in the year—and make the others so full of fear that they would not kill? No! Such a foolish policy has never worked and never will. The more you kill, the more you deny and separate, the more will they seek another form and way of life, however *blindly* and unconsciously. And out of what can they weave a different life, out of what can they mold a new existence, living *organically* in the same town and cities, the same neighborhoods with us? (333–34, emphases mine)

The dialectic Max presents here echoes the entire thematic and stylistic paradox that makes up *Native Son*. In Max's exhortation resonate the symbolic, antithetical meanings of *black* and *white*, the sun and the snow, and the figurative function of the wall or the "white looming mountain." The greater the hostility Bigger faces and the greater the obstructions aimed at subduing him, the more determined he is to force a life for himself. That he does not murder Mary purposely reflects what Max sees as the blind, unconscious, organic instinct for life characteristic of all animals.

Reinforcing Wright's synthesis of the figurative elements dominant in Books 1 and 2, Max's speech contrasts the blindness which militates against understanding the black and white worlds to the "light of reason" needed to lessen the severity of the problems that beset the inhabitants of both worlds. Max's first reference to light comes quite early in his address: "I say, Your Honor, that the mere

act of understanding Bigger Thomas will be a thawing out of icebound impulses, a dragging of the sprawling forms of dread out of
the night of fear into the light of reason, an unveiling of the unconscious ritual of death in which we, like sleep-walkers, have partici-
pated so dreamlike and thoughtlessly" (324). "A thawing out of
icebound impulses" alludes to the snow which has been shown to
represent the white world's insensitivity. Max's point is that these
impulses result from the blindness (or dreamlike state) unchal-
lenged by the "light of reason." He juxtaposes both fear and blindness to light or insight. The "unconscious ritual of death" (Bigger's
murder of Mary) is an inevitable outcome of the interaction between two people who are strangers to each other's emotions in a
world such as the one Max describes. A sleepwalker caught in the
throes of a trance, Mary makes herself vulnerable to Bigger, and he,
a sleepwalker too, kills her.

Light becomes an important image as this speech continues.
Max uses the word *light* to suggest the need for change in the
white world: "But did Bigger Thomas really *murder?* . . . I ask the
question in the *light of the ideals* [emphasis mine] by which *we*
live" (335). The phrase *light of the ideals* refers to the illusions of
morality and virtue (Cirlot 179) that veil the horror and corruption
of a Jim Crow society. Attempting to show that Bigger's needs and
drives are no different from those of any other man, Max requests
that the judge refrain from analyzing Bigger in the "light of sympathy" and in the "light of injustice." Such a reaction, he says, only
results in a sense of guilt indistinguishable from hate. The word
light, then, illuminates the hate and shame, guilt and fear common
to all people. Since it is natural for both groups—Black and white—
to "kill that which evoked in them the condemning sense of guilt"
(329), Max asks the court to evaluate Bigger's guilt in the "light of
this new reality"—the connection between the commonality of
all men and women and the role white society plays in Bigger's
predicament.

The ironic relationship between Bigger's dilemma and white

society's accountability for it culminates in Max's terming Bigger's murderous deed "an act of *creation.*" Max refers to the sun—which shares an affinity with *light* in its connotation of spiritual strength—to emphasize Bigger's confrontation with his destiny: "Excluded from, and unassimilated in our society, yet longing to gratify impulses akin to our own but denied the objects and channels evolved through long centuries for their socialized expression, every sunrise and sunset make him guilty of subversive actions. Every movement of his body is an unconscious protest" (335–36). This reference to the sun clinches Wright's adroit interweaving of the recurring image patterns discussed earlier into the fabric of Max's address. Clearly, here the sun represents the audacity and creative force behind Bigger's actions.

Max's physical demeanor and his first comment to Bigger after the speech are quite telling. With "tired," "sunken" eyes and a "bowed" head, Max says to Bigger as they take a brief recess before Buckley's summation speech, "I did the best I could" (339). Max obviously knows that his eloquent words will not save Bigger's life. If we read his speech merely as obtrusive commentary that disrupts the narrative, we miss another essential element of Wright's irony. For Wright was far too scrupulous an artist to slip carelessly into gratuitous diatribe sacrificing the tour de force performance of the novel up to Max's address. Obviously, Max's speech is as significant an expression of his personality as are his comments to Bigger during their discussion. Max is indeed a product of a world in which nothing is as it should be. In other words, his speech leads us to believe that he is the one character in the novel capable of understanding Bigger. But because his experiences separate him emotionally from Bigger, he too remains aloof. His resigned attitude and the superficial liberalism that motivates him reflect a subtle condescension which denies Bigger's humanity.

Sharply contrasting with Max in every possible way, Buckley is a perfect representative of the hostility and insensitivity connoted elsewhere in the novel by the snow and the word *white.* In the same way that Max's demeanor reflects his attitude toward his mission, Buckley's manner as he rises to address the court characterizes him as a predator convinced that he has trapped his prey:

> Bigger turned his head and saw Buckley rise. He was dressed in a black suit and there was a tiny pink flower in the lapel of his coat. The man's very look and bearing, so grimly assured, made Bigger feel that he was already lost. What chance had he against a man like that? Buckley licked his lips and looked out over the crowd; then he turned to the judge. (340)

In his black suit, Buckley evokes the same feelings of fear and humiliation associated with the color black in previous scenes. His formally festive attire and jaunty manner suggest that he too has a self-serving interest in Bigger's trial. His histrionics in the courtroom become a part of his campaign for reelection as State's attorney. The speech he delivers supplements his well-planned theatrics during the pretrial statement. His opening the window so that the judge can hear the shouts of the crowd and his bringing the furnace from the Dalton home into the courtroom so that a young woman can crawl inside demonstrate his intent to stir the emotions of the court.

Also strictly aimed at arousing emotions, his address chronologically traces the steps of Bigger's actions from the day he entered the Dalton home to the day of his capture. In a carefully orchestrated narrative he avoids the intellectual rhetoric characteristic of Max's plea. In fact, Buckley manipulates Max's description of Bigger as an animal with a succession of malicious epithets he knows will exacerbate the hate that the court already feels for Bigger. Phrases like "human scum," "black shadow of death," "half-human black ape," "black lizard," "black mad dog," "sly thug," "sub-human killer," "hardened black thing," "human fiend," and "rapacious beast" inundate Buckley's seven-page address and capture the attitude toward Bigger held by the mainstream that Buckley represents.

Buckley constantly refers to Bigger's blackness in order to re-

inforce in the mind of the court the barriers that separate Bigger
from white society. His vituperative underlining of Bigger's race
proves to be merely one means by which he exploits the Jim Crow
codes that deny Bigger's humanity. Describing Mary as "one of the
finest and most delicate flowers of our womanhood" (341), he alludes to the most sacred of the Jim Crow laws. This social code
which forbids intimate relationships between a Black man and a
white woman becomes the climax of Buckley's address. As he outlines Bigger's every move that led up to and followed Mary's death,
he shrewdly prepares the court for his histrionic, zealous, vivid in-
terpolation of the murder scene:

> My God, what bloody scenes must have taken place! How
> swift and unexpected must have been that lustful and mur-
> derous attack! How that poor child must have struggled to es-
> cape that maddened ape! How she must have pled on bended
> knee, with tears in her eyes, to be spared the vile touch of this
> horrible person! Your Honor, must not this infernal monster
> have burned her body to destroy evidence of offenses *worse*
> than rape? That treacherous beast must have known that if
> the marks of his teeth were ever seen on the innocent white
> flesh of her breasts, he would not have been accorded the high
> honor of sitting here in this court of law! O suffering Christ,
> there are no words to tell of a deed so black and awful! (344)

Buckley's every word is strategically aimed at implanting in the
mind of the court the picture of Bigger as a dangerous animal that
threatens the well-being of the white world.

He ends his response to Max's address by attacking the idea that
Bigger's murder was an instinctive "act of *creation*." Further inter-
polating the evidence against Bigger, Buckley asserts that Bigger
burned Mary's body to destroy the obvious signs of rape. Consequently, he concludes, both the rape and the murder were planned.
His inversion of Max's salient points demonstrates that he and
Max represent two extremes of the same world view. For Bigger's reality—that which distinguishes him as a human being—lies somewhere between Max's ideological, theoretical interpretation of his

personality and Buckley's vituperative depiction of him as an animal. Thus Max, symbolizing reason, and Buckley, representing emotions, demonstrate the imbalance that occurs in the human personality when drives and desires impede empathy.

When Max visits Bigger after the governor denies the appeal, Bigger's stark acceptance of his own reality destroys Max's veneer of understanding what it means to be Bigger Thomas. Stimulated by Max's previous questions, the events of the trial, and his determination to understand his past, Bigger struggles to communicate with a fellow human being before his death by attempting to impose the reality of his being upon Max. Frustrated by the superficial reaction he gets from Max, he fights for the words "to break down the wall of isolation" between them. As Bigger quells the anger he feels for Max, a pale bar of sunshine suggests Bigger's new spiritual strength and Max's shallowness, portending the exchange of roles that occurs between them:

> Max rose and went to a small window; a pale bar of sunshine fell across his white head. And Bigger, looking at him, saw that sunshine for the first time in many days; and as he saw it, the entire cell, with its four close walls, became crushingly real. He glanced down at himself; the shaft of yellow sun cut across his chest with as much weight as a beam forged of lead. With a convulsive gasp, he bent forward and shut his eyes. It was not a white mountain looking over him now . . . this new adversary did not make him taut; it sapped strength and left him weak. He summoned his energies and lifted his head and struck out desperately, determined to rise from the grave, resolved to *force upon Max the reality of his living.* (353, emphasis mine)

This rich passage makes clear the irony of Bigger's spiritual growth. Although he is surrounded by "four close walls" and is prisoner of that haunting "white looming mountain," he discovers an emotional strength that eluded him when he was physically free. The bar of sunshine that falls across Max's "white" head deepens Bigger's awareness of Max's dispassionate interest in the reality of his life.

From this point on, as revealed by the yellow sun that cuts across Bigger's chest like a beam forged of lead, Bigger assumes the role of an emotional aggressor. During the course of this last talk with Max, Bigger shows the depth of self-knowledge that comes from his bouts of contemplation. In a tour de force effort, he bombards Max with questions as Max responds with the same kind of theoretical, distant rhetoric he used in the courtroom. When Max condescendingly says "y-you've got to b-believe in yourself," Bigger finally accepts that forcing the reality of his living upon Max is impossible. For the first and only time in the novel, Bigger laughs. Bigger's deepened awareness of how his past coalesces with his present situation climactically sharpens the difference between Max's idealism and his own bleak realism:

> Sounds funny, Mr. Max, but when I think about what you say I kind of feel what I wanted. It makes me feel I was kind of right. . . . I ain't trying to forgive nobody and I ain't asking for nobody to forgive me. I ain't going to cry. They wouldn't let me live and I killed. Maybe it ain't fair to kill, and I reckon I really didn't want to kill. But when I think of why all the killings was, I begin to feel what I wanted, what I am. . . . (358)

When Bigger says "I ain't trying to forgive nobody and I ain't going to cry," he has finally reached the middle ground between the extremes of fear and terror. Max, like the hostile Buckley and the blind, philanthropic Daltons, cannot empathize with Bigger. He backs away from Bigger with "compressed lips." And after Bigger exclaims "But what I killed for, I am," Max's wet eyes are "full of terror" as he "groped for his hat like a blind man," keeping his face averted from Bigger as he leaves the cell to walk down the corridor.

Unable to confront the horrifying consequences of Bigger's tragic actions, Max rejects Bigger in this final scene. Max's repudiation of Bigger confirms that Max delivered his speech to the judge out of a sense of duty rather than from sincere concern for Bigger's life. His "fine" words bring him no closer to accepting Bigger as a fellow human being than Buckley's invectives. In fact, Max and Buckley serve as bookends representing the extremes of a white society psychologically victimized by its own social and economic dicta. Examples of Wright's skill at characterization, Buckley's and Max's speeches reveal that in the eyes of the white world Bigger is a mere object. Buckley, representing mainstream America, and Max, representing the "liberal" Communist party, both use Bigger to enhance their political careers. Having previously accepted the white world's image of himself, Bigger in this last scene understands a deeper level of his own blindness—the futility of looking outside the self for affirmation. For he had thought that Max's speech and questions meant that Max actually understood his feelings and actions. Bigger now sees that Max is as alienated from him as is Buckley or any other representative of the white world. Totally alone, then, Bigger achieves tragic equilibrium from a final, personal attempt to induce uninducible empathy. "It is in acting out his own personality, in realizing his selfhood unto death, that [Bigger] finds redemption and deliverance" (Jaspers 44). While Max remains blind in life, Bigger gains insight as he awaits his death. "The self-confident, keen-eyed reasoner [Max] fails; he does not go beyond limited truths of fact. The blind seer [Bigger] who must be led about has the long vision; he inherits a tradition, and sees the inescapable truths that lie beneath all present situations" (Heilman, *This Great Stage* 22).

Epilogue

Bigger and Max's initial relationship and the content of Max's speech suggest the historical dilemma Blacks face in America. The role reversal between Max and Bigger and Bigger's revelation, however, emphasize the need for those in the Black world to take control of their own lives both physically and psychologically, regardless of the price. In its execution of this tragic theme, *Native Son* charts Bigger's growth from darkness into light, from innocence into experience, and from ignorance into knowledge. Through suffering, Bigger learns that existence itself is inherently paradoxical. At the same time that each person is an integral embodiment of the scheme of things, we are still unequivocally locked inside our own consciousness. Wright beautifully captures this isolation in an image Bigger has as he begins to understand the ambiguity of human existence:

> Standing trembling in his cell, he saw a dark vast fluid image rise and float; he saw a black sprawling prison full of tiny black cells in which people lived; each cell had its stone jar of water and a crust of bread and no one could go from cell to cell and there were screams and curses and yells of suffering and nobody heard them, for the walls were thick and darkness was everywhere. (306)

Wright's point, suggested by the image of an isolated "black sprawling prison full of tiny black cells," is that although Blacks are entrapped by racism, they must not become so engulfed psychologically that racial dicta become the controlling factors in their lives.

The sublimity of *Native Son* lies in Wright's ingenious dramatization of the entrapment characteristic of human consciousness. For at the same time that Bigger is subjected to the powerful forces that demand his submission and thus contrive a difference between him and white society, he and the rest of the black world must be perpetually aware that they—like all other humans—possess a consciousness and self-worth that is naturally independent of outside stimuli. Ironically, the attributes that imprison Bigger and the rest of us inside our individual realities are the very distinctive features that evoke the empathy of a shared human consciousness.

Native Son, then, describes a world in which the natural order of things is so inverted that its inhabitants live in mutually exclusive environments that induce the malaises of either too much self-effacement or excessive self-assertion. Unfortunately, taking its cue from Wright's sharp rebuke of racism and its banal effects, too much of the criticism on *Native Son* begins and ends by belaboring Wright's role as social critic. Embodying both the same kind of liberalism as that reflected in Max's speech and the internalization of racist strictures that defines the characters in the novel, the criticism on *Native Son* has reacted more to Bigger's murder and burning of Mary Dalton than to the beauty behind Wright's craft. Most of the works that treat the novel approach it as though it were a political treatise or a propagandistic tract rather than a work of art.

Wright, however, believed that Black writers had a responsibility to merge their roles as social critics and creative artists. In "Blueprint for Negro Writing," he addresses the autonomy of craft and its relationship to subject matter:

> Negro writers should seek through the medium of their craft to play as meaningful a role in the affairs of men as do other professionals. But if their writing is demanded to perform the social office of other professions, then the autonomy of craft is lost and writing detrimentally fused with other interests. The limitations of the craft constitute some of its greatest virtues. If the sensory vehicle of imaginative writing

is required to carry too great a load of didactic material, the
artistic sense is submerged.

The relationship between reality and the artistic image is
not always direct and simple. The imaginative conception of a
historical period will not be a carbon copy of reality. (47–48)

Interestingly enough, criticism that insists on seeing a direct relationship between Bigger Thomas's personality and Richard Wright's
shortsightedly treats Wright's work as if it were a carbon copy of
his own life. Such an approach ignores the real beauty of imaginative art to which Wright refers in the passage above, where he
holds that the limitations the craft of writing places on the artist
constitute some of the greatest virtues of creative art. In other
words, reality, the phenomenal world, is changed on the blue guitar
of the imagination. The artist, of course, takes his cue from the
real world, but his finished product reflects the embellishing of his
or her creative vision.

The tragic artist's most important distillation is the choice of
the tragic action that thrusts the hero into his fate. As is characteristic of life, the very act that Bigger intends to save his life—his
carrying Mary to her room—is the event that catapults him into
his fate. Figuratively, Mary Dalton represents the most sacred code
of a Jim Crow society. And Bigger symbolizes the fear and dread of
those forced to live a life of submission to Jim Crow laws. Hence
Wright's creative imagination plots the inevitable consequences of
an encounter between these two antithetical forces. The irony inherent in Bigger's actions synthesizes form and meaning in the
novel. Like Oedipus's murder of his father, Bigger's murder of Mary
is paradoxically inadvertent and preordained. Although he does not
intend to kill her when he places the pillow over her face, the time
has come when his extreme fear and rebellious temperament be-
tray him.

The structure of the novel (the arrangement of parts that result
in the ironic reversal of roles between Bigger and Max), Bigger's
ambiguous personality, and the paradoxical nature of the image

patterns all function integrally as a well-orchestrated discord that becomes harmonized in Bigger's suffering as his consciousness grows. The complexity of Wright's symphonic characterization of Bigger reaches a crescendo in the rhythmical repetition and inter-locking relationship between the sentence patterns, the colors black, white, and yellow, the image of the wall, and the metaphors of the snow, the sun, and blindness. The polarity expressed in these weblike linguistic cords synthesized in Max's speech captures the tension in Bigger's psyche, a tension that evokes the awe and power responsible for the success and lastingness of *Native Son*.

Works Cited

Alexander, Margaret W. "Richard Wright." *New Letters* 38 (Winter 1971): 182–202.

Allen, Walter. *The Modern Novel*. New York: Citadel Press, 1953.

Baker, Houston A., Jr. "Racial Wisdom and Richard Wright's *Native Son*." In *Long Black Song: Essays in Black American Literature and Culture*. Charlottesville: University Press of Virginia, 1972. Rpt. in *Critical Essays on Richard Wright*, 66–81. Ed. Yoshinobu Hakutani. Boston: G. K. Hall, 1982.

Baldwin, James. "Everybody's Protest Novel." *Partisan Review*, June 1949. Rpt. in *Notes of a Native Son*, 9–17. New York: Bantam Books, 1955.

———. "Many Thousands Gone." *Partisan Review*, November-December 1951. Rpt. in *Notes of a Native Son*, 18–36. New York: Bantam Books, 1955.

Baldwin, R. E. "Creative Vision of *Native Son*." *Massachusetts Review* 14 (1973): 378–90.

Baron, Dennis E. "The Syntax of Perception in Richard Wright's *Native Son*." *Language and Style* 9 (Winter 1976): 17–28.

Bentley, Eric. "Melodrama." In *The Life of the Drama*. New York: Atheneum, 1964. Rpt. in *Tragedy: Vision and Form*, 217–31. Ed. Robert W. Corrigan. San Francisco: Chandler Publishing Company, 1965.

Bone, Robert. *Richard Wright*. Minneapolis: University of Minnesota Press, 1969.

Brignano, Russell C. *Richard Wright: An Introduction to the Man and His Works*. Pittsburgh: University of Pittsburgh Press, 1970.

Burgum, Edwin B. "The Art of Richard Wright's Short Stories." In *The

Novel and the World's Dilemma. New York: Russell and Russell, 1963. Rpt. in *Five Black Writers*, 36–49. Ed. Donald Gibson. New York: New York University Press, 1970.

Cirlot, J. E. *A Dictionary of Symbols.* Trans. Jack Sage. New York: Philosophical Library, 1962.

Cruse, Harold. *The Crisis of the Negro Intellectual.* New York: Morrow, 1969.

Delmar, P. J. "Tragic Patterns in Richard Wright's *Uncle Tom's Children.*" *NALF* 10 (Spring 1976): 3–12.

Ellison, Ralph. "The Art of Fiction: An Interview." *Paris Review,* Spring 1955. Rpt. in *Shadow and Act*, 167–83. New York: Vintage Books, 1972.

———. "The World and the Jug." *New Leader,* 9 Dec. 1963. Rpt. in *Shadow and Act*, 107–43. New York: Vintage Books, 1972.

Epps, Preston H., ed. *The Poetics of Aristotle.* Chapel Hill: University of North Carolina Press, 1942.

Fabre, Michel. *The Unfinished Quest of Richard Wright.* New York: Morrow, 1973.

Felgar, Robert. *Richard Wright.* Boston: G. K. Hall, 1980.

Fishburn, Katherine. *Richard Wright's Hero: The Faces of a Rebel-Victim.* Metuchen, N.J.: Scarecrow Press, 1977.

French, Warren. "The Lost Potential of Richard Wright." In *The Black American Writer*, 125–42. Ed. C. W. E. Bigsby. Deland, Fla.: Everett/Edwards, 1969.

Frazer, Sir James. *The Golden Bough: A Study in Magic and Religion.* New York: Macmillan Company, 1947.

Frye, Northrop. *Anatomy of Criticism: Four Essays.* Princeton: Princeton University Press, 1957.

Gibson, Donald. "Richard Wright: Aspects of His Afro-American Literary Relations." In *Critical Essays on Richard Wright*, 82–90. Ed. Yoshinobu Hakutani. Boston: G. K. Hall, 1982.

———. "Wright's Invisible Native Son." *American Quarterly* 21 (Winter 1969): 728–38.

Hakutani, Yoshinobu. "*Native Son* and *An American Tragedy.*" In his *Critical Essays on Richard Wright*, 167–81. Boston: G. K. Hall, 1982.

Hamalian, Linda B. "Richard Wright's Use of Epigraphs in *The Long Dream.*" *BALF* 10 (Winter 1976): 120–23.

Hancock, Edward. *Techniques for Understanding Fiction*. Belmont, Calif.: Wadsworth, 1972.

Heilman, Robert B. *Magic in the Web: Action and Language in Othello*. Lexington: University of Kentucky Press, 1956.

——. *This Great Stage: Image and Structure in King Lear*. Baton Rouge: Louisiana State University Press, 1956.

——. "Tragedy and Melodrama." *The Texas Quarterly*, Summer 1960. Rpt. as "Tragedy and Melodrama: Speculations on Generic Form," in *Tragedy: Vision and Form*, 245–57. Ed. Robert W. Corrigan. San Francisco: Chandler Publishing Company, 1965.

Henn, T. R. *The Harvest of Tragedy*. London: Methuen, 1956.

Howe, Irving. "Black Boys and Native Sons." In his *A World More Attractive*, 98–122. New York: Horizon, 1963.

Hughes, Carl M. *The Negro Novelist*. New York: Citadel Press, 1953.

Jaspers, Karl. "Basic Characteristics of the Tragic." In *Tragedy Is Not Enough*. Boston: Beacon Press, 1952. Rpt. in *Tragedy: Vision and Form*, 43–52. Ed. Robert W. Corrigan. San Francisco: Chandler Publishing Company, 1965.

Joyce, Joyce A. "An Overview of Ann Petry's Contribution to American Literature." *Nethula Journal* 2 (1982): 16–20.

——. "Style and Meaning in Richard Wright's *Native Son*." *BALF* 16 (Fall 1982): 112–15.

Kazin, Alfred. *On Native Grounds: An Interpretation of Modern American Prose Literature*. New York: Harcourt, 1942.

Kearns, Edward. "The 'Fate' Section of *Native Son*." *Contemporary Literature* 12 (Spring 1971): 146–55.

Kinnamon, Keneth. *The Emergence of Richard Wright*. Urbana: University of Illinois Press, 1972.

Langer, Susanne. "The Tragic Rhythm." In *Feeling and Form*. New York: Charles Scribner's Sons, 1953. Rpt. in *Tragedy: Vision and Form*, 85–98. Ed. Robert W. Corrigan. San Francisco: Chandler Publishing Company, 1965.

Larsen, R. B. V. "The Four Voices in Richard Wright's *Native Son*." *NALF* 6 (Winter 1972): 105–9.

Layman's Parallel Bible. Grand Rapids, Mich.: Zondervan Bible Publishers, 1973.

McCall, Dan. *The Example of Richard Wright*. New York: Harcourt, 1969.

Margolies, Edward. *The Art of Richard Wright*. Carbondale: Southern Illinois University Press, 1969.

Melville, Herman. *Moby-Dick or, The Whale*. Ed. Charles Feidelson, Jr. New York: Bobbs-Merrill, 1964.

Miller, Arthur. "Tragedy and the Common Man." In the *New York Times*, 27 Feb. 1949. Rpt. in *Tragedy: Vision and Form*, 148–51. Ed. Robert W. Corrigan. San Francisco: Chandler Publishing Company, 1965.

Myers, Henry A. "Heroes and the Way of Compromise." In *Tragedy: A View of Life*. New York: Cornell University Press, 1956. Rpt. in *Tragedy: Vision and Form*, 132–42. Ed. Robert W. Corrigan. San Francisco: Chandler Publishing Company, 1965.

Neal, Larry. "The Black Contribution to American Letters; Part III, The Writer as Activist—1960 and After." In *The Black American Reference Book*, 767–90. Ed. Mable M. Smythe. Englewood Cliffs, N.J.: Prentice-Hall, 1976.

Olson, Elder. "Modern Drama and Tragedy." In *Tragedy and the Theory of Drama*. Detroit: Wayne State University Press, 1961. Rpt. in *Tragedy: Vision and Form*, 177–83. Ed. Robert W. Corrigan. San Francisco: Chandler Publishing Company, 1965.

Pizer, Donald. *Twentieth-Century American Literary Naturalism: An Interpretation*. Carbondale: Southern Illinois University Press, 1982.

Raphael, D. D. "Why Does Tragedy Please." In *The Paradox of Tragedy*. Bloomington: Indiana University Press, 1960. Rpt. in *Tragedy: Vision and Form*, 187–201. Ed. Robert W. Corrigan. San Francisco: Chandler Publishing Company, 1965.

Rickels, Milton and Patricia. *Richard Wright*. Austin, Tex.: Steck-Vaughn, 1970.

Sadler, Jeffrey A. "Split Consciousness in Richard Wright's *Native Son*." *South Carolina Review* 8 (Spring 1976): 11–24.

Sewall, Richard B. *The Vision of Tragedy*. 1959; rpt. New Haven: Yale University Press, 1980.

Siegal, Paul N. "The Conclusion of Richard Wright's *Native Son*." *PMLA* 89 (May 1974): 517–23.

Walcutt, Charles C. *American Literary Naturalism, A Divided Stream*. Minneapolis: University of Minnesota Press, 1956.

Walker, Ian. "Black Nightmare: The Fiction of Richard Wright." In

Black Fiction: New Studies in the Afro-American Novel since 1945, 11–28. Ed. A. Robert Lee. New York: Barnes & Noble, 1980.

Williams, Raymond. *Modern Tragedy*. Stanford: Stanford University Press, 1966.

Wright, Richard. "Blueprint for Negro Writing." In *New Challenge* 2 (Fall 1937). Rpt. in *Richard Wright Reader*, 36–49. Ed. Ellen Wright and Michel Fabre. New York: Harper & Row, 1978.

———. "How 'Bigger' Was Born." In *The Saturday Review of Literature*, June 1940. Rpt. in *Native Son*, vii–xxxiv, 1940; rpt. New York: Harper & Row, 1966.

———. *Native Son*. New York: Harper & Brothers Publishers, 1940.

Index